Halloween
Invitation to the Occult?

By Chuck Missler

Koinonia House

Halloween: Invitation to the Occult?
© Copyright 2019 Koinonia House Inc.
Published by Koinonia House
P.O. Box D
Coeur d'Alene, ID 83816-0347
www.khouse.org

Author: Dr. Chuck Missler
Editor: Amy Joy

ISBN: 978-1-57821-812-7

All Scripture quotations are from the King James Version
of the Holy Bible.

PRINTED IN THE UNITED STATES OF AMERICA

Table of Contents

Ch. 1:   The Last Day of October. 1

Ch. 2:   Spiritual Doorways 5
         Samhain 6

Ch. 3:   All Hallow's Eve in America 15

Ch. 4:   Mars 19

Ch. 5:   Dangers of the Occult. 29

Ch. 6:   Doctrines of Demons 39

Ch. 7:   Martin Luther 47

Ch. 8:   Ghosts. 51

Ch. 9:   Reincarnation 59
         Reincarnation 62

Ch. 10: Witches and Witchcraft 65

Ch. 11: Satan 71

Ch. 12: The Witch at Endor. 77

Ch. 13: UFOs 83

Ch. 14: Our Heavy Artillery 93

Endnotes. 103

About the Author 107

Chapter 1
The Last Day of October

Every year on the last day of October, American children paint their faces, color their hair, don gowns, capes and fuzzy suits, and traipse about from door-to-door collecting bags of candy. Their parents join them, visiting parties and high school haunted houses. Together, they carve crazy faces on pumpkins, cover apples with caramel, and work to win contests for the scariest or most creative costumes.

But why? How did this holiday originate? This night of orange and black offers opportunities for spooky fun, parties with Chex mix and candy corn, and faces wet from apple bobbing. It also offers opportunities for involvements that are genuinely dangerous as people willingly meddle with the occult when they would otherwise never do so. Every year, Christians are left wondering exactly how to handle this holiday that focuses so much on death.

We might not see witches' cauldrons bubbling in local caves or Druids marching circles in the park, but it's still easy to find remnants of our pagan past in the day-to-day walk through our world. Our days of the week and the months of the year are largely named after pagan gods from Roman and Teutonic traditions. We even find aspects of those old days at Christmas – the time of year we've dedicated to honoring the birth of our Lord Jesus Christ. I think most of us are sensitive to the fact that we are immersed in a pagan culture, and it's become fascinating, and disconcerting, to watch as the world grows increasingly more open to the dark side.

Ancient pagan traditions have leaked through the centuries into the present day. The custom of kissing someone under the mistletoe can be traced back to druid beliefs about the connection of that plant to sexual potency. The term "druid" originally referred to a priest of the oak cult, by the way. Easter is the season we commemorate the death and resurrection of Christ, but all that business of chicks, baby rabbits, and eggs ties back to the Babylonian fertility religions and the goddess Astarte or Ishtar, from which "Easter" gets its name. The egg was a fertility symbol that originated in debauched fertility cults. We think of Easter egg hunts as fun activities for children. The original cult practices were anything but child-friendly. If we understand the rabbit as a symbol of fertility, we can understand how both eggs and rabbits became associated with Easter. Cadbury might give us bunnies that lay treasures of gooey chocolate wonder, but that strange idea that we take for granted - an Easter bunny hiding eggs - hearkens back to these ancient practices.

Our culture is filled with the vestiges of ancient paganism. The custom of giving out cigars at a baby's birth may hail from the times when ancient Mayan fathers would blow tobacco smoke toward the sun god as an offering of thanks for a newborn child. June is a lovely time to hold weddings, so it's no coincidence that June was named for Juno, the Roman goddess of marriage. Most aspects of the American wedding ceremony can be traced to ancient pagan customs, including the bride's white dress and veil, the exchanging of wedding rings and the father's giving away the bride. Our childhood tooth fairy, strangely enough, can be linked to efforts to hide personal physical items, like teeth, from practitioners of Voodoo (or Hoodoo). To connect a Voodoo doll to a person, a piece of his or her clothing or fingernail clippings, a lock of hair or tooth were incorporated into the doll. People hid any teeth that fell out to keep them from being used by the Voodoo priest for curse rituals. The culture in which we live is a smorgasbord of cultural influences handed down from the ancient world, just as the English language is a mixture of Anglo-Saxon, Germanic, and Latin languages. (The word smorgasbord, for instance, is Scandinavian.)

We can celebrate Christmas and Resurrection Sunday with hearts devoted to Jesus Christ, turning the focus away from the pagan roots of these seasons and giving honor to our Lord. However, Halloween seems to have little to redeem it. As Bible believing Christians, we get confronted with this particularly pagan celebration, and it should be giving us some difficulties. Once a year we face the dilemma, the problem, the burden of how to approach this holiday called Halloween, the evening before the historical Christian holiday of All Saint's Day. We can shrug off Halloween as a costume party, a time for kids to dress up and collect candy. We can let them enjoy the harmless spookiness of an autumn evening. However, there's more to Halloween than we realize, and it's a time when dangerous opportunities arise for our children to make their acquaintance with the occult.

Chapter 2
Spiritual Doorways

Halloween generates cash flow. According to estimates by the National Retail Federation, consumers spent $8.4 billion on Halloween in 2016 and $9.1 billion in 2017.[1] Half of Americans will decorate for this festival – compared to the 80% who decorate for Christmas. All Hallow's Eve is not just a quaint reminder of days gone by; it's now the third most popular cause for throwing parties, just behind the Super Bowl and New Year's Eve. Halloween is big business, and I wish that's where it ended. It's always a difficult time for Christians and especially those with children.

How should parents deal with this time of year? Dressing up in costumes is fun! Eating candy is fun! What harm is there in that, besides tummy aches and cavities?

I'm going to suggest that Halloween is an exceptionally treacherous time. It glorifies horror, but that's not all there is to it. It glorifies all things scary, dangerous and dark, and there are a variety of seemingly harmless involvements associated with Halloween that can serve as spiritual doorways. That's where the biggest dangers lie. We call these "entries" into the occult, and some can prove tragic for the unwary.

The English word "occult" comes from the Latin *occulere* which means to conceal or hide. The purpose of the occult, in whatever form you want to frame it, is to deceive.

If we were living in Israel during the Exodus, it wouldn't cause much stir if we argued that the world was flat. We'd be wrong, but it wouldn't cause much debate - except among the most educated astronomers. However, if we engaged in anything smacking of astrology, the Law of Moses required that we be put to death. If someone held a séance and attempted to speak with the dead, the Israelites were ordered to execute that person. Capital punishment was decreed by God for witchcraft, sorcery and communicating with familiar spirits, because these things all allowed demons—with all their deceptive, corrupting influences—access into the lives of the children of Israel.

Samhain

While Halloween has flourished as an American holiday, its roots are found in ancient Britain and Ireland. The Celtic festival of Samhain ("sow-in") was observed on October 31, the end of summer in Cornwall. On both the Celtic and Anglo-Saxon calendars, November 1 marked the New Year. The date was connected with the return of the herds from pasture. Laws and land tenures were also renewed at that time. In Ireland, all the apples had to be harvested before October 31, because it was believed that wicked Irish fairies known as *púca* would spit on the apples after that date. It was one of the most important times of the year in the Celtic culture, but we discover it was also one of the most sinister times of the year.

The Celts were people who radiated out from central Europe during the Middle Ages and possibly earlier, settling in Spain, France and the British Isles. The Celtic people engaged in what we'd now call the occultic arts. They worshipped nature, ascribing to it supernatural qualities. The Druids were a priestly class of the Celts, and when we study them, we find many similarities with Hinduism in their beliefs and practices. The Celts taught reincarnation and transmigration of the soul. They taught that people can be reborn as animals. Julius Caesar gives us some insight into the Celts of his day, describing the people and their culture in his work, *Gallic War*:

> The cardinal doctrine which they seek to teach is that souls do not die, but after death pass from one to another; and this belief, as the fear of death is thereby cast aside, they hold to be the greatest incentive to valor. Besides this, they have many discussions as touching the stars and their movement, the size of the universe and of the earth, the order of nature, the strength and the powers of the immortal gods, and hand down their lore to the young men.[2]

It's interesting that the Druids and the Celts venerated memory and oral recitation so highly that they left few written records. Most of what we know about the Celts comes from the records of the Romans. Caesar describes the Celts' worship of the Roman gods Mercury, Apollo, Mars, Jupiter and Minerva. According to Caesar, the Celts believed that they descended from Dis (Pluto), the god of the dead, which he explains is why they reckon their days from nightfall to nightfall. Caesar also describes the Celtic habit of using human sacrifice to appease the gods, including stuffing giant dolls with men and setting them on fire:

> They believe, in effect, that, unless for a man's life a man's life be paid, the majesty of the immortal gods may not be appeased; and in public, as in private, life they observe an ordinance of sacrifices of the same kind. Others use figures of immense size, whose limbs, woven out of twigs, they fill with living men and set on fire, and the men perish in a sheet of flame. They believe that the execution of those who have been caught in the act of theft or robbery or some crime is more pleasing to the immortal gods; but when the supply of such fails they resort to the execution even of the innocent.[3]

According to the Roman historian Tacitus, the Druids covered their altars with the blood of their victims. The larger the number of victims, they believed, the greater the crop yield would be the following year. The Druids even used human sacrifice as a method of telling the future. Tacitus notes that human intestines were used in divination, saying, "The Druids consult the gods in the palpitating entrails of men."[4] Roman geographer Strabo describes how a man was stuck in the back with a sword, and the Druids would then interpret omens from the convulsive movements made during the victim's death struggles.[5] Diodorus Siculus describes this practice in greater detail:

> The Gauls likewise make use of diviners, accounting them worthy of high approbation, and these men foretell the future by means of the flight or cries of birds and of the slaughter of sacred animals, and they have all the multitude subservient to them. They also observe a custom which is especially astonishing and incredible, in case they are taking thought with respect to matters of great concern; for in such cases they devote to death a human being and plunge a dagger into him in the region above the diaphragm, and when the stricken victim has fallen they read the future from the manner of his fall and from the twitching of his limbs, as well as from the gushing of the blood, having learned to place confidence in an ancient and long-continued practice of observing such matters.[6]

These were the Druids, the priestly class of the ancient Celts. Their religious practices horrified the Romans, who made strides to put an end to human sacrifice. The coming of Christianity further mollified the British Isles. Yet, vestiges of those ancient rites can still be found today.

How does all this tie into Halloween? The Celts were the trunk from which Halloween grew. The Druids believed that on the last day of the old year, Samhain, the lord of darkness and death gathered the souls of the evil dead that had been condemned and forced them to enter the bodies of animals. It was believed that he would then decide which animal form they would take for the next year. The souls of the good dead were reincarnated as humans. The Druids also believed that the punishments suffered by the evil dead would be lightened by sacrifices, prayers, and gifts to the lord of death. Here we begin to find a strange link between certain Druid practices associated with Samhain and later beliefs about purgatory within the Roman Catholic Church.

The Celtic worshipers attempted to placate Samhain because of his power over the souls of the dead. On Halloween, it was believed that the separation between the realms of the living and the dead grew thin, and those who had died during the preceding twelve months were permitted by Samhain to cross over. Whether good or evil, they were permitted to visit their former places of habitation for a few hours, to associate once again with their families.

It was on these occasions that ancient fire festivals were celebrated on local hilltops. The Celts would build giant bonfires to frighten away the evil spirits. Because the souls of the dead were supposed to visit their homes that day, the annual festival acquired a sinister significance. The Celts believed that ghosts, witches, goblins, fairies, and demons of all kinds roamed about. Evil or frustrated ghosts were supposed to play tricks on humans to cause supernatural manifestations. The Celts were determined to handle the supernatural powers, and as part of the celebration, the people would don grotesque masks and danced around the bonfires to scare away those wandering evil spirits. In some cases, food was placed out for the dead to make them feel welcome. We begin to understand how those traditions reached across the ages to the celebration of the holiday today.

With the barriers between the spirits and the living so thin, Halloween was thought to be the most favorable time for divinations. The Druids would use their arts to tell the future about marriages, health, and death. It was considered the only day on which the help of the devil could be invoked for such purposes. That's one of the strange superstitions that emerges in all of this.

It's interesting to look at pagan religions throughout the world and discover that many celebrate a time when the dead return to mingle with the living. The Hindus light bonfires on their first night of Holi. The Iroquois Indians celebrated the Feast of the Dead. In Mexico, the Day of the

Dead begins on November 2. In Russia, all the witches and spirits were said to gather once a year on the Summer Solstice to hold bonfires and engage in fertility rituals. The composer Modest Mussorgsky depicted this Slavic witch's holiday in his composition St. John's Eve on Bald Mountain. It's a passionate musical composition and was featured as one of the segments in the Disney movie *Fantasia* (1940). It depicts this legend that all the witches in Russia came to Bald Mountain and reveled all night in their wicked celebrations and worship of Satan. The music eloquently portrays them disappearing as the dawn arrives.

During the Middle Ages, the Catholic Church in Europe made an attempt to oppose paganism by replacing pagan celebrations with Christian holidays. In order to offset Samhain, they created All Saints Day on November 1st as a day to commemorate all the saints of the Church. We find the first mention of a Christian celebration on November 1 during the reign of Pope Gregory III, but it was in A.D. 837 that Gregory IV ordered the general observance of All Saint's Day. The next day, November 2, was later designated as All Soul's Day, which eventually became a day designated for praying for the dead. Pagan traditions were mixed in with Christian efforts to honor the saints, and we see the results of syncretism in the holiday practices that followed. The practices of the ancient Celts were commingled with the Catholic concept of Purgatory.

By the late eighteenth century, it was customary for English Catholics to assemble at midnight on Halloween to pray for the souls of their departed friends. In northern Europe, worshippers ate special soul cakes with the promise to pray for souls to be freed earlier from Purgatory. Children and the poor would beg from door to door, "*A soul cake, a soul cake, a prayer for a soul cake!*" On All Soul's Day, cakes with images of skulls and skeletons were eaten in Sicily, and in France the day was dedicated to prayer for the dead who were not yet glorified. People ate soul cakes because they thought them to be powerful antidotes against the flames of Purgatory that might be invoked on the returning ghosts at dusk. Lighted candles were placed on the graves and in the windows to guide the dead back home.

Halloween was not celebrated in early American history. It was not widely observed until the nineteenth century, when it was introduced by the Irish Catholic immigrants who brought ancient traditions from their homeland.

The idea of Purgatory did not originate in Catholicism. Naraka is the place of temporary punishment after death in Hinduism. In Plato's Republic, Socrates tells Glaucon about a man who awoke from the dead twelve days after being killed in battle. The man described a place where the dead were judged. Some were thrown into Hell, but others suffered ten-fold for their crimes and after 1000 years were allowed into Elysium.

The Druids believed that the sinful souls of those who had died during the year had been relegated to the bodies of animals, but through gifts and sacrifices of sins could be expiated and their souls freed to claim their heavenly reward.

The one place we find no mention of Purgatory is the Bible. The Bible teaches that Jesus Christ came to take away the sins of the world, and there is no other way to get to heaven.[7] In the Old Testament, sins were paid for by animal sacrifices, but Hebrews 10 makes it clear that even those sacrifices were merely meant to point to Christ. As Hebrews 10:4 states: "*For it is not possible that the blood of bulls and of goats should take away sins.*" We cannot pay for our sins with money. We cannot pay for them with prayers. The only act sufficient to pay for our sins was already accomplished on a cross in Judea 2000 years ago, and our part is to trust in the finished work of Christ.

Chapter 3
All Hallow's Eve in America

In medieval England, the Halloween festival became known as All Hallow's Eve. The feast was abolished by the Church of England after the Reformation, but gradually a Halloween tradition became introduced into the United States by the Irish immigrants who poured into the country during the late 1800s. It gradually became a secular observance that was celebrated by many who didn't know about its religious background—and didn't care. A variety of practices developed, carried over from the ancient times and changed to fit a secular purpose in the new world.

One of these traditions is the familiar carving of jack-o-lanterns. Celebrants have long gutted pumpkins and other gourds and carved them with faces so that they give off an eerie orange glow when lit candles are placed in the bottom. It's interesting how many different ideas are used to explain the jack-o-lantern. The carved pumpkin tradition probably originated from the witches' use of a skull with a candle inside, with which they illuminated their coven meetings.

However, we do find strange legends among the Irish, including the legend of Irish Jack. Jack was presumably a stingy drunk, who tricked the devil himself into climbing a tree for an apple. Jack then cut the sign of the cross into the tree trunk, preventing the devil from coming back down. Jack forced the devil to swear that he would never come back after Jack's soul, and the devil reluctantly agreed. When Jack eventually died, he was turned away from the gates of heaven because of his life as a drunk, selfish sinner. He then went to the devil, but he also rejected Jack in honor of his promise. As Jack left hell, the devil flung a live coal at Jack and condemned him to wander the Earth, rejected from both above and below. Jack put the coal inside a hallowed-out turnip, making the first jack-o-lantern. Eventually, pumpkins replaced the turnip, especially in America where pumpkins were plentiful. That's one of the Irish legends told to children to explain what we call a jack-o-lantern. It's colorful and strange, and it makes a good story.

Americans love to dress up in costumes on Halloween. The ancient Druids dressed up like the returning souls of the dead as a self-defense. The real spirits might just think they were one of them and not bother them. The disguised Celts paraded to the outskirts of town to lead the dead souls away, and they would be greeted with a banquet-laden table at the end of the feast day.

Druid ceremonial participants also wore animal heads and skins to acquire the strength of the particular animal whose skins they wore. Typical animistic beliefs, masks and costumes were employed in traditional shamanism and other forms of animism to change the personality of the wearer to allow communication with the spirit world.

Immigrants to the United States, particularly the Irish, introduced these Halloween costume traditions, and they became popular in the late 19th and early 20th century. The night became one of mischief making instead of one dedicated to praying for the dead. Those with a sense of humor used the opportunity to play practical jokes that could be blamed on ghosts or witches. Rather than going from door to door "souling" and seeking soul cakes, children traveled through neighborhoods from house to house asking for treats. Those who didn't offer yummy foods might be rewarded with a prank or trick, because that's what ghosts and witches did: they created mischief on the living.

"Trick or treat!" the children call.

The November 3, 1927 edition of *The Calgary Daily Herald* of Alberta, Canada, reported from the *High River News*:

> Hallowe'en came and went and was observed most circumspectly in town, without the usual depredations. The greatest activity was manifested by the very young, who wandered in droves from door to door, heavily disguised and demanding "trick or treat." To treat was to be untricked, and the youthful hold-up men soon returned home bowed down with treats.

That same day, *The Blackie Times* of Alberta Canada described the Halloween festivities of the year, stating:

Halloween gave an opportunity to the young to use up some of their surplus energy which was freely taken advantage of. Threshing outfits, wagons, parts of wagons, old autos, barrels, etc., decorated the front streets and buildings were overturned, while front and back doors were invaded and inmates held up by the awful word "Trick or Treat" from the youthful invaders...

To turn the focus away from vandalism and increasingly rowdy and destructive behavior, efforts were made to turn Halloween into a time that focused on the youth. In 1965 the United Nations International Children's Emergency Fund (UNICEF) adopted Halloween as an opportunity to collect money. It became common for UNICEF to show up on doorsteps on Halloween, seeking money. It sounds like an appropriate thing, and it got some of the focus off mischief-making and onto charity. However, to me it seemed strangely appropriate for the ungodly United Nations to exploit this pagan holiday.

Chapter 4
Mars

As we proceed down the path of exploring this strange holiday, I can't resist pointing out the bizarre possibility that one of our planets is partly to blame for Halloween. As we study these ancient cultures—not just the Celts, but virtually all the ancient cultures—we discover something very strange; they all worshiped the planet Mars. We find in the folklore that these cultures worshipped the hosts of heaven, especially the planets, because they moved through the sky from night to night.

One of the ancient names for Mars was Baal, which is familiar to us from the Bible. We shrug off their beliefs and practices as ancient superstitions, yet we discover that these cultures were terrified of the planet.

Mars became synonymous with war. We use that same term even today when we speak of the martial arts. It's in our vocabulary now. We regard ourselves as a sophisticated culture as far as space and astronomy are concerned, but I imagine few of us could go outside tonight and point to the planet Mars. Venus and Jupiter are much brighter than Mars in the night sky today, yet these ancient cultures were terrified by the planet Mars and consistently regarded it as the god of war. Why? One possibility is that the planet Mars interfered in their lives.

As we study ancient calendars, we discover some strange things. A number of ancient calendars that I've been able to track down were built around 360-day years and 30-day months until about 701 B.C.. The Chaldeans, the Egyptians, Hebrews, Greeks, Phoenicians, Chinese, Hindus, Carthaginians, Etruscans, Mayans and the Teutons all based their calendars on a 360-day year. The Chaldeans used a base 60 numeral system 2000 years before Christ, handing down to us the conventions of 360-degree circles, 60-minute hours, and 60-second minutes. The Assyrians used a 360-day calendar and a 3600-day decade. The Egyptian year included 12 months of 30-days each. Most cultures around the world observed 12 months of 30 days until 701 B.C.. In 701 B.C., for some reason, that all changed. The Hebrews added a month every three years or so, the Egyptians and Chaldeans added a few days per year.

The Bible continues to count the year as 360 days all the way through Revelation 11:2-3. The solar tropical year has been measured to 365.2422 days long, so it appears that something happened in history to add 5.25 days to what had once been a 360-day year.

In his 1950 book *Worlds In Collision*, Immanuel Velikovsky tried to reconcile these mysteries - that the earth had a universal climate at one point in history and the 360-day year was so widespread. He used what can be called comparative mythology rather than astronomy to come up with ideas about the history of some planets – for instance, that Athena had sprung from the head of Zeus, and therefore Venus must have arisen from the planet Jupiter. These things have been discounted by astronomers, because Velikovsky's celestial mechanics don't conform to Newtonian celestial mechanics. His interpretations of the Athena birth might have been incorrect, but he points out very interesting correlations between ancient mythologies are still worth contemplating. There seemed to be more than four visual naked-eye planets, and Earth's magnetic poles appear to have reversed. Velikovsky offers some peculiar ideas to explain these things in his very readable book.

Why did so many ancient calendars all change from 360 days to 360+5, or start adding an extra month every few years? Some historians just assume the ancients were ignorant and finally corrected the problem after enough time went by, and they realized that the solar year didn't coincide with the lunar year. I don't buy that. The ancient peoples were capable astronomers who could count. They would have quickly figured out that they were losing 5.25 days each year, and it wouldn't have taken thousands of years to realize it.

There are some strange theories, and in recent years as we've refined our understanding about planetary orbits, we've recognized that orbits can resonate just like sound waves do with tuning forks. They can interact with each other and thus have a tendency towards resonance.

In the early 1970s, researchers Don Patten, Ron Hatch, and Loren Steinhauer speculated that the Earth originally took 360 days to orbit the Sun, while Mars took twice as long: 720 days – with all manner of implications.[8] In the models, Saturn and Jupiter and Venus were also factors, but I want to keep it simple for this discussion. Patten, Hatch, and Steinhauer's models imply that Mars would have made a near pass-by with the orbit of the Earth every 108 years. Each time the near pass-by took place, energy transferred from one planet to the other until finally, in 701 B.C. the energy transfers between Earth, Venus, and Mars were so great it destabilized the resonance of the orbits, changed the orbits of Mars and Earth enough that we don't experience those close visits anymore. Earth now has an orbit of 365.25 days, and Mars has one of 687 days. Mars has only 10% the mass of Earth, and in that final transfer of energy, Earth slowed just 5.25 days per year, and Mars gained 33 days.

If this idea is correct, Mars once passed near Earth on a predictable basis, which coincided with a series of catastrophes in the ancient past, recorded in a variety of ways. Our study *The Mysteries of the Planet Mars* goes into these issues in more depth.[9]

I became interested in this partly because it impacts what is called the "long day of Joshua" in Joshua 10. In this story, Joshua tells the Sun and Moon to stand still for a day, and they do. If the Earth's rotation were just to halt for a day, brutal disasters would have taken place across the entire world. If there were a near pass-by of Mars at that time, however, and the Earth's very orbit were changing, the Moon and Sun might have appeared to stand still while Earth's rotation was maintained. Something even more extreme took place in Hezekiah's day around 701 B.C.: the shadow on the sundial went backward 10 degrees.[10] It's monstrous to suggest that the Earth's rotation reversed just to give King Hezekiah a sign that he would be healed. However, this story might indicate that Earth's very orbit was in the process of a brutal shift.

These stories are colorful, but they explain certain things – like the ancients' great fear of Mars. If Mars drew near enough to Earth every 108 years that its red surface could be seen with the naked eye, and if that near approach were accompanied by natural disasters due to the gravitational pull between Earth and Mars, there would certainly be cause for terror. It sounds like the stuff of science fiction, but it seems to be corroborated by a guy named Jonathan Swift, the Irish satirist who we know best by his story *Gulliver's Travels.*

We're all familiar with Swift's tale about the Lilliputians, the little people who tied up Gulliver when he landed on their shores during his first voyage. We think of these as children's stories, but Swift's intent was a very bitter satire on the government in London. The Irish did not have a warm feeling for England, and Jonathan Swift wrote this fantasy as a mechanism to poke fun or to satirize the situation in London at the time. In his third voyage, Gulliver encounters a place called Laputa. The astronomers in Laputa brag that they know about the two moons of Mars, which the astronomers in London don't know about.

Galileo reported seeing four of Jupiter's moons with his telescope in 1610, as well as Saturn's rings. In 1781, William Herschel discovered Uranus and then the moons of Uranus in 1787. It took until August 18, 1877 for Asaph Hall to discover the two tiny, dark moons of Mars through the new telescope at the U.S. Naval Observatory. The scientific world was shocked to learn that Mars did have moons after all.

The outer moon, Deimos, is less than eight miles in diameter and the inner moon Phobos is only about fourteen miles across. Both of the moons have a low albedo, which means they don't reflect light well. Phobos is the darkest object in our solar system, reflecting about 3% of the light that hits it. It's tiny—just one hundredth of the width of our Moon—and it orbits Mars in 7.65 hours, several times in one 24.623-hour Martian day. Deimos, the outer Martian moon, orbits the planet every thirty hours and eighteen minutes. We can observe these things now, but there is no way for anybody in the 1700s to have seen those two moons, let alone describe them in detail.

Yet, 150 years before Asaph Hall spied the moons of Mars, Jonathan Swift's characters in Laputa describe the two moons of Mars. In chapter three of the *Voyage To Laputa*, Swift says:

> They have likewise discovered two lesser stars, or satellites, which revolve about Mars; whereof the innermost is distant from the center of the primary planet exactly three of his diameters, and the outermost, five; the former revolves in the space of ten hours, and the latter in twenty-one and a half; so that the squares of their periodical times are very near the same proportion with the cubes of their distance from the center of Mars;

Swift wrote this book 151 years prior to the actual discovery of the two moons of Mars. The astronomical world did not take the Laputans' descriptions of Mars' moons seriously, of course, and then Asaph Hall saw the two moons of Mars and astonished everybody. Swift's descriptions are not precise; Phobos circles the planet in seven hours and thirty-nine minutes, not ten hours, but Swift's details were certainly close enough to make one wonder. What's more, Phobos is drawing closer to Mars at a rate of 1.8m every hundred years, so its orbit was longer in the past. Swift's descriptions seem much closer than we'd expect of pure guesswork.

I've wondered whether Jonathan Swift had access to records that he assumed were just legend, and he drew upon them to add color to his satire. Today the closest Mars can theoretically approach Earth is 33.9 million miles, but before the resonance was destroyed, Mars might have approached close enough for early astronomers to measure the orbits of its moons – so close that it terrified the Earth's inhabitants.

How does all this fit into the celebration of Halloween? Halloween isn't the winter solstice, when the days start to lengthen again. It's not the time when little chicks are born and the trees and flowers start blossoming after the death of winter. Why did the Celts call November 1st the New Year?

Mars would always have made its near pass-by around the end of October or the end of March, so it's interesting that the worship of Mars seems to be associated with these times of the year. The Romans had their new year in March, and March is named after Mars. As we look at these things, we begin to understand the Bible's admonitions against worshiping the hosts of heaven. The ancient cultures took planetary movements seriously, and God warns the peoples that this behavior is a form of idol worship, a form of demon worship. Yet it's reasonable to assume they focused on Ba'al or Mars around October 31 because these occasional run-ins with the red planet scared them badly and caused all kinds of natural disasters.

It's an interesting speculation.

Chapter 5
Dangers of the Occult

There are obviously many superstitions surrounding Halloween, and it has become a time when people engage in occultic activities that they would otherwise avoid. On Halloween, playing with elements of the darker side is seen as spooky, scary fun—and the results can be disastrous for the naïve.

For many years, Halloween has been the appointed day for The Salem Psychic Fair and Witches' Market in good old Salem Massachusetts, in which attendees are encouraged to meet real witches and psychics. The fair advertisements offer Tarot card readings and palm readings, crystal ball scrying and readings of past lives. They offer visits with spirit mediums and others who can tell fair-goers if they have their own angels or spirit guides. A normal county fair might include events like "Calf Roping" and "Barrell Racing" but the events at Salem on Halloween include "Speaking to the Dead" and "Conjuring Spirits."

The fact that we can have public gatherings like this demonstrates how far from the Bible we have fallen as a culture. These are practices that God very specifically forbids—on pain of death.

There is no middling about it. The LORD told the Israelites to absolutely stay away from these practices, and they were part of the reason that God had the Israelites replace the Canaanites.

> *Regard not them that have familiar spirits, neither seek after wizards, to be defiled by them: I am the LORD your God.*
>
> Leviticus 19:31

> *And the soul that turneth after such as have familiar spirits, and after wizards, to go a whoring after them, I will even set my face against that soul, and will cut him off from among his people.*
>
> Leviticus 20:6

> *There shall not be found among you any one that maketh his son or his daughter to pass through the fire, or that useth divination, or an observer of times, or an enchanter, or a witch, Or a charmer, or a consulter with familiar spirits, or a wizard, or a necromancer. For all that do these things are an abomination unto the LORD: and because of these abominations the LORD thy God doth drive them out from before thee.*
>
> Deuteronomy 18:10-12

In our world today, pastimes like visiting psychics or palm readers are portrayed as harmless fun, but that's foolish. Dabbling in the occult is like spiritually playing in the freeway. Even Shakespeare understood this. In his play *Macbeth*, the title character and his friend Banquo are returning from battle when they are met by three witches. The witches offer the two men prophecies, among which are that Macbeth will soon become the Thane of Cawdor, and afterward the king. Sure enough, messengers of King Duncan soon arrive and inform Macbeth that the king is bestowing on him the title Thane of Cawdor. Macbeth elbows Banquo and reminds him that the witches were right! Banquo is more cautious, and he makes the following observation:

> *And oftentimes, to win us to our harm,*
> *The instruments of darkness tell us truths,*
> *Win us with honest trifles, to betray's*
> *In deepest consequence.*[11]

Satan has a way of mixing truth with poisonous lies that can easily lead to our destruction. The Bible warns us against even rubbing elbows with diviners or those who consult familiar spirits. These can be dangerous spiritual "doorways," and the entities we meet are most likely to be the deceptive enemies of our souls, whose whole desire is to lead us away from God, to infect us and dig hooks into us and use us for their diabolical purposes. At first, they might offer their victims words of truth, but only as a trick. In the end, they betray them "in deepest consequence," as Banquo warns Macbeth.

What results from Macbeth's heeding the witches, after all? He does become the king by murdering good King Duncan, and the rest of the play resounds with misery and bloodshed and, ultimately, Macbeth's violent death.

We as Christians should have some real problems with occultic practices, and we certainly should teach our children the dangers of occultic activities, of giving Satan the smallest foot in the door of our lives. On the other hand, it's hard to tell our kids, "No candy for you!" while all the other children are out having fun dressing up and going door to door collecting Snickers and Milky Way candy bars. As Christians, where do we draw the line?

Many churches today provide the neighborhood kids with "harvest" parties on Halloween, complete with costumes and candy and fun, but with a different focus. Some take the opportunity to teach kids about the dangers of occultic practices, to explain to them about spiritual warfare. It's a great night for educating our young people on the reality behind Paul's words in Ephesians 6 – that our true enemies are spiritual and not physical. Satan is prowling around like a lion, seeking those he can devour,[12] but we have all authority in Jesus Christ, and we are protected by His blood. Some congregations gather together to make Halloween a night of worship and praise. There are a lot of things that can be done on Halloween that allow the kids some interesting fun while protecting them from the evils associated with the pagan background of the holiday.

There are evil spirits out there seeking souls to deceive.

We have a problem in our culture, however, as fewer families read and know the Bible. Halloween parties can include supposedly innocent games that lead to serious spiritual entanglements. One of the things that shows up around Halloween are the Ouija boards, which can be found on the shelf in department stores. The word "Ouija" comes from the French and German words for "Yes." It's treated as an amusement, and of course there's nothing intrinsically wrong with a piece of plywood or carboard with some letters and a little pointer. Sometimes these things are used for practical jokes, but because it's often used as an attempt to communicate with the dead, it becomes an "entry" for evil spiritual entities.

In 1971, William Blatty published a book that was made into the 1973 movie *The Exorcist*, based loosely on true events that took place in 1949. At the time the movie came out, I was on Walter Martin's board, and Walter was deeply offended by the movie. He set out to discredit William Blatty but discovered that Blatty had done his homework. The novel is based on an amalgam of several true case studies, but primarily on a boy in the Washington D.C. area. In the movie, we find a girl portrayed, but she becomes demon-possessed after playing with a Ouija board, through which she meets a spiritual entity that calls itself Captain Howdy. Not "Devil" or "Dagon, lord of the underworld" but friendly, nice sounding, "Captain Howdy."

I find it interesting that the copyrights for the Ouija board are owned by Parker Brothers, which was originally founded in 1883 by George S. Parker in his hometown of Salem, Massachusetts. Just a notable tidbit.

Many people glance at the astrology columns carried in most popular newspapers as a sort of an amusement, a curiosity. Our lives, our personalities, our futures are not written in the movements of Jupiter and Venus, and while most people don't take astrology seriously, it still gives a hat tip to the old star worship that the Bible forbids.

In 1965, Walter Martin published a book called *Kingdom of the Cults*, which I consider relevant still today. It's one of the definitive volumes on comparative religions. Walter was an expert, and the book has become a classic. He did a follow up work that focused on occultism, which he aptly named *The Kingdom of the Occult*.

I have an interesting story to tell about Walter. We were doing speaking engagements and taping them, because we knew we might be facing spiritual warfare. We did the series on the occult in St. Andrews, and I was trying to get Walter free of the crowd because it was after 10:00 pm on the west coast, which for Walter's body was

1:00 am, and he hadn't eaten. So, I wanted to get Walter out of there. One of my associates brought a couple of people along, a wife and a husband and a psychiatrist, and he said, "These people have to talk to Walter tonight."

I said, "Larry, it's just too late. We've got to spare Walter all this stuff."

Walter overheard this and said, "Oh, I'm available. Why don't we just meet at my room?"

When we pulled up at the inn and the other couple's car pulled alongside us, Walter knew that something was up. He said, "Hey, let's pray."

All of us, four grown men and this girl, ended in Walter's room, and that inn experienced an exorcism that you'd think came out of the book of Acts. At first, there were many voices and violent reactions, and then a feigned peace. I don't think the psychiatrist was a Christian, but he recognized that he was up against something that he didn't know how to deal with, which is why they sought out Walter. Well, it got to the point at which the girl seemed to be fine, but the psychiatrist somehow knew it wasn't over. In the end, we had a classical exorcism. A year or two later we ran into the husband and wife, and the husband confided to us that he had a whole new woman given back to him by the Lord Jesus Christ.

I recommend *The Kingdom of the Occult*, because it doesn't approach this spiritual battlefield from a merely scholastic point of view. Walter has dealt with real spiritual warfare. He's cast out demons through the power of Jesus Christ. He's even performed exorcisms over the phone. I want to take an excerpt from this book to give you the flavor of it, but also to illustrate the danger of dabbling in occultic activities:

> For the next four hours, I conducted an exorcism over the telephone! The pastors would talk to the demons, get back on the phone to tell me what the demons said and then go back in the room and talk to the demons again. Now this may sound crazy to you, but it was very real to those men: Christian gospel preachers.

> We found out eventually that she had been into the heart of the New Age movement— associated with a half dozen or more New Age organizational ideas and concepts. It turned out she had 100 demons in her! I told them to get a tape recorder or no one will ever believe it happened. They commanded the demons in the name of Jesus Christ to identify themselves, every single one of them. They actually recorded their names and some of them were very interesting. They were the names and the terms of the world of the occult because she had been into all of these movements. She was spewing out the names of demons associated with actual movements.

> Four hours later the Holy Spirit cast the last of the demons out of that girl in the name of

Jesus. A pastor called me back and said, "It's over. They're gone! Praise the Lord!"

I said, "Yes, praise the Lord!"

And then he said, "She wants to talk to you."

She came to the phone and said, "I have been possessed for the last few years. I couldn't help myself, and I didn't know where to turn. I kept going to these cults and to these occultic groups and each time there would be more demons instead of less. I finally decided to come here. I want to thank you for staying on the telephone and helping the ministers. I want to praise and thank God that I have just received Jesus Christ as my Savior. I want you to know I am free. They're gone and I love Jesus! Thank God He set me free."

The terrible danger of the occult is that people expose themselves and their children to it and are unaware of the spiritual pitfalls. When it results in the unleashing of satanic power, as in this case study, then they are totally unprepared to deal with it.[13]

There were occasions when I would travel with Hal Lindsey around southern California to various speaking engagements, just as a friend and driver. During these trips I noticed a common occurrence. As soon as we reached the church, they would usher us off to a side room or restaurant where a small group of maybe six to twelve senior elders and their wives would meet with us and provide us with food and pleasantries. However, while Hal was there to speak about prophecy, the pastors and elders at these churches did not ask Hal about prophecy. In church after church we would find the pastors wanting to confidentially explain that they had somebody in the congregation they believed was demon possessed, and they didn't know how to handle it. While prophecy was interesting, the real gut issue behind the scenes was the widespread demon aneurysm that was arising in America.

Chapter 6
Doctrines of Demons

The United States harbors the fastest growing and most highly organized body of Satanists and occultists in the entire world. The occult can include a broad collection of activities and persons, including channelers clairvoyants, psychic spiritists, diviners, gurus, Shamans, psychical researchers, Yogis, holistic healers, astral travelers, astrology, mysticism, Tarot cards, contact with the dead, and even UFOs. It's not just about straight Satanism or Satan worship. It can include the Kabbalah, Gnosticism, theosophy, witchcraft, and forms of what can be classified as serious magic, including the search for hidden knowledge.

Since the beginning, Satan has worked hard to deceive the human creations of God. God loves us, and we have great authority and power through Him. He has given us the fruits of His Spirit—love, joy, peace, patience, kindness, goodness, gentleness, and self-control—which all reflect who He is. God is love.[14] In His presence there is fullness of joy.[15] Our Lord is the Prince of Peace.[16] He has also given us gifts through His Spirit, gifts of prophecy and healing and knowledge, gifts of being great artists and musicians and mathematicians, gifts of prophetic dreams and interpretation of dreams. He has given us wonderful gifts, which we should all be exercising as members of the Body of Christ, as Paul describes in 1 Corinthians 12-14. We all need the children of God to be acting and moving in their gifts, because those gifts act as a blessing to all of us.

Satan works hard to make us believe God is not acting or is not willing to help us, and then Satan tells us that he himself provides real power. Satan is a con artist who offers a cheap, fake replica of God's gifts, and while God offers freedom and healing, Satan seeks to overpower and dominate us so that we are ultimately destroyed.

The Bible makes something very clear: there is only one true God, the Maker of heaven and earth. Isaiah states this over and over again. Any other spirit who claims to be god is a fraud – and there are a lot of fraudulent spirits out there. Psalms tells us that the gods of the nations are merely idols, and the Bible repeatedly tells us that those who worship idols and false gods worship demons. These are important concepts to understand, to get into our brains. Let's consider some verses:

> *Thus saith the LORD the King of Israel, and his redeemer the LORD of hosts; I am the first, and I am the last; and beside me there is no God.*

Isaiah 44:6

*Fear ye not, neither be afraid: have not
I told thee from that time, and have
declared it? ye are even my witnesses. Is
there a God beside me? yea, there is no
God; I know not any.*

Isaiah 44:8

*Remember the former things of old: for I
am God, and there is none else; I am God,
and there is none like me…*

Isaiah 46:9

*For the LORD is great, and greatly to be
praised: he is to be feared above all gods.
For all the gods of the nations are idols:
but the LORD made the heavens..*

Psalm 96:4-5

*They sacrificed unto devils, not to God;
to gods whom they knew not, to new gods
that came newly up, whom your fathers
feared not.*

Deuteronomy 32:17

*Yea, they sacrificed their sons and their
daughters unto devils…*

Psalm 106:37

*And the rest of the men which were not
killed by these plagues yet repented not of
the works of their hands, that they should
not worship devils, and idols of gold,
and silver, and brass, and stone, and of*

*wood: which neither can see, nor hear,
nor walk:*

Revelation 9:20

Idols are just dumb wooden and stone statues with no life inside them. Yet, the idols that the nations worship and have worshipped since the time of Babel do have evil spiritual powers behind them, and worshiping idols involves demon worship. A Ouija board is just a piece of wood or cardboard. In itself, it is nothing, and yet it can be used to summon demons.

Satan has been at work since Eden, focused on his goal of demolishing humanity. He has never stopped, and he has his minions, his legions of workers who seek to deceive and corrupt and control human beings who have stepped out from under God's protection. Every century, every other decade, he puts a different focus on the lies he spreads, but his tactics have never changed. He wants to deceive, drag down, and destroy the people for whom Jesus Christ died. Paul warns Timothy that the deception will only grow toward the end.

*Now the Spirit speaketh expressly, that in
the latter times some shall depart from
the faith, giving heed to seducing spirits,
and doctrines of devils; Speaking lies in
hypocrisy; having their conscience seared
with a hot iron;*

1 Timothy 4:1-2

Paul uses the interesting term "doctrines of devils." Where do we find doctrines of demons today? All over the place. It's easy to go down to any secular bookstore and find that one of the largest selections in that bookstore is spirituality, which includes every set of beliefs under the sun because the bookstore owners are trying to serve a market. They're going to scratch where people are itching, and one of the highest volume turnover areas is New Age paganism. The area of the bookstore which offers books on witchcraft and Satanism and pagan New Age views is much bigger than the Christian section of the bookstore. Why? Because people are buying it. The bookstores just stock what's moving. They're not making a statement. They're providing a service.

We are not teaching people well enough that these are the doctrines of demons, that they are spiritually dangerous. We would never purposely dive into a pool of cholera and *E. Coli* and Ebola pathogens. Yet Satan has dressed up the curtain to the occult to look interesting and fun, and those who go swimming in it have no clue they've jumped into spiritual filth and have made themselves vulnerable to every kind of evil spiritual disease.

Why are New Age materials selling so well? We have failed to teach the truth! Of course, deceptive doctrines have been steadily enforced by the state and federal governments through our schools - and increasingly so - but we also can't overlook the churches in America. Many churches are teaching doctrines that twist or distort or completely ignore the Word of God. We as a people rarely read the Bible or fail to recognize the Bible as the Word of God, and that has left us susceptible to every kind of deception.

According to a 2018 Pew Research study, there are a surprisingly high number of self-professed Christians who embrace at least one New Age belief. Out of every ten people from a Christian background, six believe in at least one of the following: psychics, spiritual energy in physical objects, reincarnation or astrology.[17] According to the study, even 47% of Evangelicals have accepted one of these. Only about a third of Americans believe in astrology and reincarnation, but that's still a remarkably high ratio in a nation where eight in ten people purport to believe in God.

When I was a teenager, I was blessed to fall under the tutelage of a competent Bible teacher in southern California. As an impressionable teen, I learned many of the prophetic themes that we saw taking place in the twentieth century. I saw Israel reestablished in the land and the rebirth of the State of Israel. It didn't take a lot of biblical homework to discover that this all fit together, and I could see or feel or get a handle on a lot of the things the Scripture referred to in the End Times. There was one thing I came across that bothered me: the prophecies that witchcraft and sorcery would increase in the end times.

I attended an excellent school and I benefitted from a good, technically-backed education. As a product of rationalism and the scientific age, I couldn't see how witchcraft and sorcery and all this old paganism could re-emerge. I couldn't visualize it. However, I can remember vividly in the late 1960s, as an executive back east, being startled by two things. The "counterculture" that was arising at Berkeley not only included drug abuse and loose sexual mores, but also an increased interest in witchcraft and Satanism. At the time, I thought that was a bit bizarre.

However, I was greatly surprised by another thing. As a senior executive at Ford Motor Company, I would traffic around the country talking to other senior executives of other major companies. It startled me to notice that many of the top executive officers owned books and periodicals aimed at witchcraft. I began to be conscious that the intelligentsia of the corporate boardrooms included many practicing occultists. I had always associated the occult with ignorance or superstition, and it amazed me to find these executives involved in it.

For unrelated reasons, during this time I discovered passages in the Bible that speak of witchcraft and sorcery. The English word translated as "witchcraft" in the New Testament comes from the Greek word φαρμακεία (*pharmakeia*), the same Greek word from which we get the term "pharmacy." When you and I think of sorcery, we think of the medieval literature, but the word literally has to do with the use and abuse of drugs. The link between drugs and witchcraft suddenly hit me between the eyes. It startled me enough to go back and dig out my old notes and do more homework on these things.

Witchcraft and New Age ideas have a strong draw on the people of our culture, and we need to recognize the spiritual dangers involved. We need to be aware and teach our children the dangers inherent in messing around with the dark side. God didn't command us to avoid these practices to take away our fun; He commanded it because Satan is just waiting to get his hooks into us.

It's interesting that certain slivers of secular science have been willing to acknowledge the possibility that psychic abilities are real and have tried to make parapsychology a legitimate field of research. The Rhine Research Center at Duke University has ongoing research on psychic powers. In 1965, J.B. Rhine, heavily funded by the Xerox Corporation, began the Foundation for Research on the Nature of Man (FRNM), and their work has continued ever since. The Rhine researchers operate under the assumption that psychic abilities are natural powers of the mind, and they measure physiological and bioenergetic changes in those who operate using those powers. When we dig deep, however, we tend to discover that people who exhibit these kinds of skills are getting assistance from the dark side.

Chapter 7
Martin Luther

I do want to step to one side and talk a bit about another Halloween story, one that is close to many of our hearts.

On November 10, 1483 in Saxony, a baby boy named Martin Luther was born to a coal miner. As he observed the poverty of his father, young Luther chose to pursue a different vocation. Coal mining didn't pay, so he decided to become a lawyer.

However, in 1505 an event took place that ultimately changed the world. On his way back to his studies in Erfurt after visiting his parents, Luther encountered a thunderstorm that terrified him, and he feared being struck by lightning. He made a vow in that moment that altered the course of his life: "Help!" he cried. "Dear Saint Anna! I want to become a monk!"[18]

Despite his friends and his disapproving father, Luther gave up on the law and joined an Augustinian monastery, where he applied himself so diligently that he earned a doctorate of theology in just a few years. The more he studied, the more troubled he became because he lacked personal peace. The question he repeatedly wrote in his diary was, "How can a man find favor with

God?" In search of peace, he devoted himself to an exceedingly pious lifestyle. He'd fast for ten or fifteen days at a time. When temperatures dropped below freezing, he slept outside without a blanket. He beat his body black and blue and bleeding, hoping that by punishing his flesh, he could rid himself of the thoughts and motives that he knew were not right. These were typical practices in the medieval church. Luther spent so much time confessing every tiny, paltry imagined infraction, his superior famously said, exasperated, "Look here, Brother Martin. If you're going to confess so much, why don't you go do something worth confessing? Kill your mother or father! Commit adultery! Stop coming in here with such flummery and fake sins!"[19]

Martin Luther became increasingly introspective, continually plagued by what he knew of his own depravity and sinfulness. Once while sitting at his desk, writing theology, he said he felt the presence of Satan so tangibly that he grabbed his bottle of ink and hurled it across the room at where he thought the devil was standing. The ink crashed into a wall and left a permanent stain.

Finally, Luther met a wise monk who told him to read Habakkuk. Just like all of us, Habakkuk pondered over the common question, if God is good, why does He allow suffering? Why does He allow evil to continue? As Luther read through Habakkuk, he was captured by the second part of verse 2:4, which declares, "*the just shall live by his faith.*" That verse changed Luther's life. He ceased doing penances to try to justify himself. Instead, he returned to the University of Wittenberg and went on to explore this revolutionary idea of justification by faith.

Meanwhile, Luther came to be horrified by the sale of indulgences as a means to raise money for the Pope and his building projects. He denied that people could be saved from torments in Purgatory by donating money. This extortion by the Roman Catholic Church inspired Luther to write out a list of ninety-five discussion points on matters he thought the Church needed to reconsider.

And this is where Halloween comes in. On October 31, 1517, Luther drove a stake into the heart of the many unbiblical concepts that had crept into the Church. I sincerely doubt he understood the firestorm he would inspire when he nailed his Ninety-five Theses to the castle church door at Wittenberg, Germany. This act, which Luther meant to foster some doctrinal introspection, sparked one of the most important series of events in modern history, the Reformation. Soon Europe would split into Protestants and Catholics, those who wanted the Church to change and those who defended the status quo.

In the end, the Catholic Church excommunicated Luther as a heretic, but they didn't kill him. He went on to write commentaries that are classics today, and he wrote hymns like

"A Mighty Fortress is Our God." He translated the entire Bible into German, an accomplishment that remains a literary classic of the German language.

Luther didn't invent opposition to the Roman Catholic Church, and it had not been his intention to cleave Christianity into pieces. Priests who came before Luther had protested the abuses in the Church. The Oxford scholar and priest John Wycliffe had spoken against bad doctrine and had willfully translated the Bible into English. The Czech priest Jan Hus had preached for reform, and they burned him at the stake for it. The tinder had been building throughout Europe for well over a century, and on October 31, 1517, Martin Luther sparked a flame when he nailed those Ninety-five Theses to a door and set Europe on fire.

Chapter 8

Ghosts

Before I go any further, I do want to make an important point. We have victory over the works of darkness through Jesus Christ. We do not have to fall victim to the evil works of Satan. The God of the Universe has given us authority over these destructive spiritual beings, and they are already defeated through the blood of Christ. That's just a reminder. In the last chapter of this book, I offer suggestions on alternative things that kids can do on Halloween, but I also focus on the power we have through spiritual warfare.

One of my biggest reasons for writing this book is to point out the danger of naively walking into the domains of demons and opening ourselves to their influences or believing their lies. Satan does an excellent job of appearing innocent, and our culture is filled with innocuous-looking material that provides subtle deceptions, giving us the wrong ideas about how the spiritual world actually works.

One of the problems we have is the ignorance of Hollywood. There are some fun movies out there—moving, enjoyable movies, that are just plain wrong. We have people portraying incorrect ideas about life after death and the spiritual world, and unless we are educated through the Bible, these wrong ideas get lodged in our heads as though they're reality. The romantic movie *Ghost* with Demi Moore and Patrick Swayze touched a lot of people, but it's just not correct. Audiences loved *The Sixth Sense*, and we were all stunned by the surprise ending. It was a well-directed movie that grossed nearly $700 million dollars worldwide, but it presents an incorrect idea about dead people. There's a common idea that the dead are wandering around, unable to pass over to the other side until certain issues are resolved, and that's not biblical. The characters that haunt Ouija boards are constantly pretending to be dead people, but it's a lie. They are deceptive spirits seeking access to us.

In Luke 16:19-31, Jesus described two men who had died. The poor man Lazarus went straight to the "Bosom of Abraham," and the wicked rich man went to hell, where he suffered in flames. Father Abraham explains to the dead rich man that there is a great gulf between them, and Lazarus cannot pass over it to give the rich man water. What's more, when the rich man begs Abraham to send Lazarus back to the earth to speak to his rich brothers, Abraham says, "*If they hear not Moses and the prophets, neither will they be persuaded, though one rose from the dead.*" Lazarus would have had to rise from the dead to speak to them.

Paul says that to die is to depart and be with the Lord.[20] When Stephen is being stoned in Acts

7, he prays, "Lord Jesus, receive my spirit."[21] Peter tells us that the unrighteous are held for the day of judgment,[22] as the angels who sinned are chained in hell, awaiting judgment day,[23] and Jude agrees.[24] Paul tells us that to be absent from the body means to be present with the Lord.[25]

The New Testament recognizes the existence of spirits that can plague human beings. Jesus spends a large part of His ministry casting out unclean spirits. After Jesus has risen from the dead, the disciples are afraid that He's a spirit, and He reassures them, saying:

> *… Why are ye troubled? and why do thoughts arise in your hearts? Behold my hands and my feet, that it is I myself: handle me, and see; for a spirit hath not flesh and bones, as ye see me have.*

Luke 24:38-39

Jesus then eats some fish and honeycomb with them, so that they can know that He's a real, live human being. The word for spirit or ghost throughout the New Testament is πνεῦμα (*pneuma*), which has the idea of "wind" or "breath." It's the spirit in a man that animates the body. The Spirit of God is called the Holy Spirit, but there are also plenty of unclean spirits that possess and torment people. Lest we be confused, though, we find a variety of occasions in which "unclean spirit" is used synonymously with "devil" from the Greek word δαιμόνιον (*daimonion*) from which we get our word "demon."[26] Humans have spirits, but in no case are these wandering spirits treated as the spirits of the departed.

Grieving widows, people who have recently lost parents or friends, are all easy targets for mediums. We've all been in that position, feeling deeply the pain of separation after the loss of a loved one. It's natural to want to know if our dearly departed are okay in the afterlife. Some mediums are charlatans taking advantage of the grief-stricken. The most dangerous mediums are not the charlatans, but those who have true access to spirits. Unclean spirits can know things about our loved ones during their lives. They can give information nobody else should know, but they can also use that to betray us in deepest consequence.

Christian ministries aimed at the Mormons have a tough time, because many of the Mormons will describe rituals in which their departed dead came and appeared, and it's exceptionally challenging to tell someone who has had that experience that the visit was demonic counterfeiting.

There's a whole body of literature about poltergeists. The word comes from two German words: *poltern* which has to do with being noisy, and *Geist* for "ghost" or "spirit." Thus, a poltergeist is a noisy ghost. Poltergeists continue to knock open cupboards and break dishes to this day, and there are multitudes of books on the subject.

They don't usually possess evil trees that attack people, as in the 1982 movie *Poltergeist*, but they do throw things across the room.

There are typically three views regarding poltergeist activity.

View 1: Poltergeists and other ghosts are the roaming spirits of the dead. That's a widely held view by many authors and experts. It is non-biblical. The demons promote this idea as a deception, because the Bible teaches that the only spirits running around, aside from the Holy Spirit himself, are angels or unclean spirits. When people in the Bible die, they are either in the pit, in Sheol or Hades – the place of the dead, awaiting judgment – or they are with the Lord. That's it.

View 2: Poltergeists are a psychological phenomenon resulting from a human psychic ability. In other words, people are throwing things around with their mind power, whether consciously or not. In his 1991 book *The Holographic Universe*, Mike Talbot describes poltergeist activities that followed him his entire life, even from early childhood. He'd always assumed these were the results of his own psycho-kinetic abilities. Unfortunately, people may not be aware of the demons inside and around them. They are so used to these spirit beings, they don't know the difference. However, psychic abilities are always connected to spiritual sources. The Holy Spirit can give believers gifts of knowledge and prophecy, and Satan's minions can give their hosts extra-sensory knowledge. Satan loves to counterfeit God's righteous power.

Without the spiritual intervention, however, psychic abilities are impossible. In Acts 16:16-19, we find Paul and Silas in Philippi, where they come across a young girl with psychic abilities. Once they cast out the demons inside her, she loses her powers—which causes her owners to lose their source of income. This upsets them, and they have Paul and Silas arrested.

View 3: Poltergeists are caused by demons. This final view is supported by the Bible, in which disembodied spirits do violence—for instance, they jump into a whole herd of swine and run them into the water. [27] It's also supported by the fact that poltergeists behind Ouija boards and hauntings can be removed by prayer and taking authority over them in Jesus' name.

I used to operate out of Big Bear in southern California, and on Wednesday nights I would do a Bible study at Calvary Chapel Costa Mesa. I would come down off the mountain on Tuesday and stay at Hal Lindsey's house, then go do a men's Bible study in the morning at the Marie Calendar's and then Bible study on Wednesday night in Costa Mesa. This was my cycle.

Hal had a special guest room in his comfortable home, and he and Kim were very gracious to receive me. Those were precious days. One particular Tuesday night, they were doing some remodeling in my normal room, so they moved me to a never-used room down the hall. As I was getting ready for bed, Kim gave Hal a funny look and asked, "You're not going to tell him?"

Hal said, "Well, I was just going to see what would happen." Hal leveled with me and explained that nobody had ever survived an entire night in the room. When their daughters stayed in that room, they always had strange experiences, so one night Hal decided to sleep in there and try it out. He said he woke up in the middle of the night floating a foot off the bed, and it scared him to death. Hal had thought he'd stick me in there, and he wanted to give me no warning and just see what happened. Nice guy.

When I went to go to sleep, though, we knelt by the bed and prayed against the forces of darkness. Candidly, nothing happened that night. It was uneventful, and I think Hal and I were both a bit disappointed the next morning when I gave my progress report.

They've since completely remodeled that room and moved from that house, and I suspect its troubles are a thing of the past. However, based both on experience and on the Bible, it seems that demons tend to be territorial. They can be confined to certain geographies. We find in Daniel 10 that there are spiritual beings tied to certain empires – like the Kingdom of Persia or the Kingdom of Greece.

I suggest that if you buy a home, or each time you move into a new place, consider walking the property line and exercise authority over your dwelling place. We don't know the spiritual history of any piece of real estate, and we don't know what practices have taken place in any of the rooms in our homes.

When Calvary Chapel acquired a new place at Murrieta Hot Springs for a new conference center, I asked Chuck Smith if he had walked the property line and prayed over the place, because that location had an interesting history. Chuck turned to me and said, "Every day. Every day."

The Bible warns us strongly against efforts to talk to the dead, calling this activity an "abomination." There's a good reason for this: we can't talk to the dead. We can only get messed up with evil spirits who pretend to be our dead relatives.

> *There shall not be found among you any one that maketh his son or his daughter to pass through the fire, or that useth divination, or an observer of times, or an enchanter, or a witch, Or a charmer, or a consulter with familiar spirits, or a wizard, or a necromancer. For all that do these things are an abomination unto the LORD: and because of these abominations the LORD thy God doth drive them out from before thee.*

Deuteronomy 18:10

Truth matters. The lies the enemy spreads have real consequences.

Chapter 9

Reincarnation

We find in our culture today a warming to the idea of reincarnation and past lives. Oscar winning actress Shirley MacClaine made the news in the early 1980s when she promoted her views on reincarnation and past life regression. She believes she's been a gypsy, a pirate, and an Indian princess who communicated telepathically with elephants. She claims to have had a multitude of past lives, including several in Atlantis. These are alluring things to say. Even people who don't believe in reincarnation can perk up and wonder what exactly she saw in those supposed past lives in Atlantis. That's foolish, though. MacClaine doesn't know how those "memories" truly entered her head.

MacClaine has embraced the full range of New Age philosophical beliefs. She not only promotes reincarnation and open sexual relationships but also communication with spirit guides and aliens, and that's where she should have been cautious long ago.

1 John 4:1-3 tells us to test the spirits. There are plenty of spirits out there, but we are warned

not to trust any that deny the deity of Jesus Christ, who is the Word of God made flesh.[28]

We might not realize this, but the very effort to remember past lives can expose people to evil spiritual influence. Those who want to find out about their past lives undergo either self-hypnosis or hypnosis under the guidance of a hypnotherapist. In both hypnotism and transcendental meditation, people work to relax and empty their minds, opening themselves to suggestions from outside of themselves. The mind is incredibly important, and we are never to give up control of our own thoughts.

Even when we are operating in the gifts of the Holy Spirit, we maintain in charge of the gifts God provides us. As 1 Corinthians 14:32 tells us, "*The spirits of the prophets are subject to the prophets.*" The Holy Spirit never "takes over" us. We still have total control over ourselves when He leads us. However, the evil spiritual powers are not such gentlemen.

It's foolish to purposely remove all thoughts from our minds and move into a hypnotic state, because that leaves us exposed to outside control. We are not supposed to open up our mind to allow others things in, to accept their words, their ideas as memories. The Bible tells us that we are responsible for what we think, for the thoughts we allow to take hold.

> *Casting down imaginations, and every high thing that exalteth itself against the*

> *knowledge of God, and bringing into*
> *captivity every thought to the obedience*
> *of Christ;*
>
> 2 Corinthians 10:5

It's interesting that Shirley MacClaine has received information from what she calls "star people." When she first mentally saw Atlantis in the ocean, she said, "The star people told me that it was the center of all energy for the Earth and was connected to each land mass, which would one day become countries." [29] It is honestly worth noting how often New Age beliefs and encounters with "aliens" go hand-in-hand.

We often think of children as innocent and untouched, but unless they are under the protection of Christ and the Holy Spirit, they are just as vulnerable, if not more so, to enemy influence. The Bible describe several instances of child possession.[30] Children's imaginations can be powerful, and it can be difficult to know if a child's invisible friend is just a game of pretend or whether something more malevolent has revealed itself to the unsuspecting tot. Poltergeists often follow people even as little children. Those who believe in past lives hold up as evidence young children who describe events in other towns in other places as their own memories. The enemy can take advantage of kids too, and we have to make sure we keep our children spiritually protected through prayer.

The Bible absolutely rejects the idea of reincarnation. There's no karma bank in the sky, and there are only two ways to pay for our sins. Either we pay for them, or Christ pays for them. We get one go at life, and that's it.

Hebrews 9:27 tells us, *"And as it is appointed unto men once to die, but after this the judgment."* We don't get a dozen or a thousand chances to get it right. Life isn't like the 1993 movie *Groundhog Day*, in which Bill Murray has countless chances to win the heart of Andie MacDowell. This means that we need to know our Savior right now. Any one of us could get hit by a truck tomorrow and die, and that's it. There are no do-overs. Yet, the lie of reincarnation gives people a false hope. They may not appreciate the importance of seeking God and His forgiveness right now before it's too late. Knowing the truth matters.

I don't want to dwell here long, but there is a little poem about reincarnation that I like by the old curmudgeon cowboy Wallace McRae:[31]

Reincarnation

What is reincarnation? A cowboy asked
his friend.
It starts, his old pal told him, when your life
comes to an end.
They wash your neck and comb your hair and
clean your fingernails,
And put you in a padded box away from
life's travails.

The box and you goes in a hole that's been dug
in the ground.
Reincarnation starts in when you're planted
'neath that mound.
Them clods melt down, just like the box, and
you who is inside.
And that's when you begin your transformation
ride.
And in a while the grass will grow upon your
rendered mound,
Until some day, upon that spot, a lonely flower
is found.
And then a horse may wander by and graze
upon that flower
That once was you, and now has become your
vegetated bower.
Now, the flower that the horse done eat, along
with his other feed,
Makes bone and fat and muscle essential to
the steed.
But there's a part that he can't use and so it
passes through.
And there it lies upon the ground, this thing
that once was you.
And if perchance, I should pass by and see this
on the ground,
I'll stop awhile and ponder at this object that
I've found.
I'll think about Reincarnation and life and death
and such,
And come away concludin', why, you ain't
changed all that much.

Chapter 10
Witches and Witchcraft

The spirits behind the occult are real. They are active, they're malevolent, and they're out to do us harm. Seances and astral projection, past life readings and psychic readings and Tarot cards should not be dismissed as colorful pastimes or casual games. They are serious. They are used to create misinformation by very powerful sentient beings whose skill and weaponry is primarily in the realm of deception. Even if they fail to possess those who mingle in their midst, they provide ideas that lead people away from Christ, away from appreciation for their sin and need for a Savior.

There are more witches today in England and America than there ever have been before. There are many Christians today who will come to the defense of the Harry Potter series, justifying it as a fun epic story with no *real* witchcraft in it. That may be so, but it has successfully removed the stigma associated with witches and witchcraft, which is dangerous. Harry Potter might be an exciting story that doesn't teach children any real spells, but it has given many children the desire to be a witch. There are children all over the place now that long to go to school at Hogwarts.

They might not be able to do that in real life, but they can certainly go learn to be witches. Witchcraft is real.

Wicca and witchcraft have grown in popularity since the 1970s. Wicca is seen by many as a harmless Earth-first, nature loving religion. Practicing witches go out to be one with nature and enjoy Mother Earth and celebrate solstices and equinoxes and full moons. It's a modernized version of an old system of worship. The Wiccans are essentially getting back to very ancient pagan basics with nature and mother goddess worship and the use of magic arts and rituals from eastern occultism. They deny that they have anything to do with Satanism or devil worship, and most embrace the Wiccan Rede, which states "If it harm none, do what you will."

Yet, Wiccans are seeking to access powers in the self or in nature and to draw that power into themselves. They do not believe in a personal God, but they do seek to tap into spirits and powers in order to manipulate circumstances in their lives. They believe that the deity is within, that we can be gods and goddesses. The deity is both within and without. They do not believe in evil or sin, which leaves Wiccans very susceptible to evil spirits who have dressed themselves to look good. Wiccans purposely open the door for spirits to come in without knowing the true nature of those spirits.

We all want to be able to fix the problems in our lives. We all want to have more power, more control. That's a common human desire. The allure of witchcraft is that it offers people the power to effect changes through rituals and magic. Of course, all that comes with a price. Unclean spirits do not offer their assistance for free and inviting them into one's life is a good way to get chained and ultimately controlled by them.

> *Regard not them that have familiar spirits, neither seek after wizards, to be defiled by them: I am the LORD your God.*
>
> Leviticus 19:31

God's way is the opposite. He asks us to humble ourselves when we come to Him, to recognize both our own sin and His power and authority. His purposes for us are the opposite of Satan's as well. Satan seeks to enslave us, but God's great desire is to set us free from the power of sin and death over our lives and to make us His children and heirs.

Charles Manson is dead now, but I suspect his name will remain notorious for many years. I remember well the events surrounding his murder of Sharon Tate and the bloody mess of slaughters Manson and his "family" members committed in the summer 1969. Manson's girlfriend Susan Atkins was also arrested and kept in solitary confinement, but she asked to see me because she had heard my Bible study tapes.

Susan Atkins previously followed Anton LaVey, the head of the Church of Satan, but had come to give her life to the Lord Jesus Christ. She wrote a book called *Child of Satan, child of God,* and naturally I read her book and did a little homework in preparation to go see her. On the book, they had a picture of her when she was arrested: a frail, gaunt, haggard, tragic looking figure. When I met with her, the difference in her physical appearance startled me; I found a gal who was petite, attractive, fresh, crisp and clean. I was prepared for a change, because she'd come to the Lord Jesus Christ, but I was startled to realize how pervasive the change had been.

Satan tears down and destroys. He might not make his move immediately but, in the end, he always seeks to humiliate and devastate his victims.

Many witches, and people in general, believe that there are good witches and bad witches, as though we live in the land of *The Wizard of Oz.* They believe in white magic, which is good, and black magic, which is evil. The problem is that whether the witch has good intentions or not, witchcraft itself is always evil. It's not because the witch wants evil, because that might not be the case; the witch might want good things. The problem is that witchcraft seeks to access powers that are not of God, which only leaves one alternative. This re-packaging of witchcraft, with the deception of white magic versus dark magic, is one of the reasons for the success of witchcraft in Western culture. Few people want to choose evil;

but it's easy for even well-meaning people to be deceived if they don't know the truth.

Kelly Segraves, the one-time administrator of the Creation-Science Research Center of San Diego, often gave talks and, somehow, he was invited to be a speaker at the annual Los Angeles witchcraft convention. Kelly thought it would be a great idea to present the Gospel at this convention. He developed a talk that started out spooky, but his ultimate aim was to present the Gospel. However, when he stood up before this crowed, every time he started to speak, he heard a loud screaming. He kept looking around, trying to figure out where it was coming from, and he noticed that the audience wasn't looking around like he was. He finally realized the audience couldn't hear it, and he knew he was in over his head. Dealing with demons isn't something any one of us should get into unless the Holy Spirit is calling us to it. As Walter Martin used to say, "I've never met a demon I really liked."

Halloween is one of the Wiccan religion's most significant nights of the year. It was a high day for the Druids and it's still a high day today. It's a day Wiccans can ask off from work as a religious holiday. Tragically, the witches are messing with powers they don't understand, and they have turned their back on the true source of life and peace and love.

There is a day of judgment, and in that day, the works of the occult will not be able to save anybody. Isaiah warns Babylon of this in Isaiah 47. Babylon, the city of Nimrod the warrior who led the great rebellion against God after the Flood, is portrayed as the city of witchcraft and sorcery. Isaiah 47, Jeremiah 50-51, and Revelation 17-18 all describe a time of judgment that will mean the utter destruction of Babylon, and there will be no saving her. Isaiah tells Babylon:

> *Stand now with thine enchantments, and with the multitude of thy sorceries, wherein thou hast laboured from thy youth... Let now the astrologers, the stargazers, the monthly prognosticators, stand up, and save thee from these things that shall come upon thee. Behold, they shall be as stubble; the fire shall burn them; they shall not deliver themselves from the power of the flame: there shall not be a coal to warm at, nor fire to sit before it.*

Isaiah 47:12-14

Chapter 11
Satan

Ultimately, we know Satan is the power behind all false religions, witchcraft, idolatry, and the occult. It's therefore important for us all to understand who Satan really is. There is a glut of misunderstanding floating around in our culture about Satan, He exists, first of all. He is an actual, real being and not just an idea. He is not equal to God but is a created being who will one day be judged and thrown into the lake of fire.[32] He is not ugly or red, and he doesn't go around with horns and a forked tail. In fact, Satan was created beautiful, and the Bible tells us he can appear as an angel of light.[33] Satan was an apostate angel who fell from heaven, and Jesus tells us He saw it happen.[34] Jesus calls him the "prince of this world" three times in John.[35] In Revelation, John calls him the dragon, "*that old serpent, called the Devil, and Satan, which deceiveth the whole world…*"[36] Jesus explains the character and nature of Satan when speaking to the Pharisees. He pulls no punches when he says:

Ye are of your father the devil, and the lusts of your father ye will do. He was a murderer from the beginning, and abode

*not in the truth, because there is no
truth in him. When he speaketh a lie, he
speaketh of his own: for he is a liar, and
the father of it.*

John 8:44

He is the father of lies. Satan has a kingdom,
and his kingdom is hostile to Christ's kingdom.[37]
These aren't just ancient ideas or labels for past
superstitions. These are dynamic active realities.
Today, Satan's goal is to deceive the whole world,
and he knows he has only a short time to do so
before he is stopped forever.[38] He is the spirit who
now works in the children of disobedience.[39] The
Bible tells us a great deal about Satan, and we cover
his rise and fall in-depth in our *Angels* series.[40]

When we walk through our lives, there are
some who are open to the Gospel, and there are
some who are currently pawns of the enemy. They
might not remain forever so – Paul reminded
the Ephesians that they were once controlled by
that same evil spirit before they knew Christ.[41]
However, until they are under the blood of Christ
and led by the Holy Spirit, they may still be pawns
of this malevolent entity, so we need to be cautious.
Satan is seeking to deceive the whole world. That's
why it's vital we commit ourselves to prayer every
day. We pray for our families and our homes
and any ministry we hold dear. One of the most
powerful things we can do is commit all things
precious to us in prayer to the protection of God.

> *Behold, I send you forth as sheep in the*
> *midst of wolves: be ye therefore wise as*
> *serpents, and harmless as doves.*

Matthew 10:16

When a ministry is set up, there are often around-the-clock prayer vigils. Those involved take time slots, just like soldiers with their scheduled time to take watch. The ministry is constantly bathed in prayer and worship, especially during critical engagements. Satan seeks to sow the seeds of fear and doubt and error in the church. If he can turn us against each other, he will do it. Who is the accuser of the brethren? That's Satan, the accuser.[42] It's remarkable how Christians arrange themselves in circles and then fire at each other. Divide and conquer is an old tactic, and Satan uses it expertly to this day. If we're aware, though, we can recognize the tactic and pull out our reinforcements. A daily schedule of prayer and worship in any ministry – or family – not only provides protection, it puts the prayer warriors on the offensive rather than merely the defensive.

Satan is capable of possessing men, and he took over Judas in John 13:27. According to 1 Peter 5:8, he prowls around like a roaring lion seeking people he can devour. His key abilities are deception and cunning. He's highly intelligent and he understands how human beings work. He's got a lot of power, don't think he doesn't, but his power is limited. We have the ability and authority to break down the gates of hell, and that's something Satan works overtime to hide from us. He loves to terrify us and make us cower. He loves to make us feel defeated and helpless when we have the power to go into his kingdom and flush it out. He knows how to fight the battle, but he also knows that his time is short.

Satan craves honor and glory. He wants us to bow to him and give him the worship due only to God. He tried to get Jesus to bow down and worship him during the temptation in the desert.[43] That was always his failure. It was the reason he fell in the first place: pride.

> *How art thou fallen from heaven, O Lucifer, son of the morning! how art thou cut down to the ground, which didst weaken the nations! For thou hast said in thine heart, I will ascend into heaven, I will exalt my throne above the stars of God: I will sit also upon the mount of the congregation, in the sides of the north: I will ascend above the heights of the clouds; I will be like the most High. Yet thou shalt be brought down to hell, to the sides of the pit.*

Isaiah 14:12-15

Satan is not all-powerful. He is powerful, but not all-powerful, and his days of tormenting the world are limited. As we watch the world succumb to his lies all around us, we have the ability to take the battle to him and to reclaim our homes and communities. We can send him running. As James 4:7 tells us, *"Submit yourselves therefore to God. Resist the devil, and he will flee from you."*

If we start the battle, though, we need to see it through by dedicating ourselves to daily prayer and thanksgiving, living our life in love with Christ. We need to cover all our loved ones in prayer, since Satan will try to distract us by attacking them. We need to seek the Lord's guidance in tearing down the strongholds of the enemy, praying that God's Spirit and His spiritual armies will come in and take dominion.

Satan doesn't win. He is doomed, and he knows it.

Chapter 12
The Witch at Endor

In 1 Samuel 28, we find a bizarre chapter in the history of Israel. Israel's King Saul has been long preoccupied with the pursuit of his rival David and has neglected the growing Philistine threat to Israel. The Philistines decide to undertake a new strategy and set up their camp in Shunem near the Jezreel Valley south of Mount Gilboa. There they can use their chariots to cut Saul off from the northern tribes, and Saul sees the danger and is terrified. The Israelite forces are camped about five miles to the south of Mount Gilboa, and Saul doesn't know what to do.

During this time, David has gone to live with the Philistines. They trust him because King Saul wants David dead, and they have no clue David goes out and destroys entire groups of Canaanites in his spare time.[44] David plays the part of the loyal Philistine subject so convincingly, he's even been appointed as bodyguard to Achish, the king of Gath.

Meanwhile, the prophet Samuel has died, and the LORD is not answering Saul through the priests or the prophets. Saul is full of fear over the Philistines, and the LORD is not giving him any counsel about what he should do. Saul has removed all the mediums and wizards from the land, which was good, but we see here the typical weakness of Saul in doing what's right. He's chased the occultists out of the land, but now that he must go fight the Philistines and God isn't answering him, he decides he'll go see a medium. If the other prophets can't help him, he figures maybe he can speak to the dead Samuel and get some advice.

Saul has a problem. He disobeys God over and over again. In 1 Samuel 15, Saul did not obey God to utterly destroy everything pertaining to the Amalekites. He feared the people and kept some of the spoil rather than just doing what God said. For this, God told Samuel that He was through with Saul. Samuel grieved all night over it, because he loved Saul, but in the morning Samuel told Saul the bad news. It was over for him as king:

> *Behold, to obey is better than sacrifice,*
> *and to hearken than the fat of rams. For*
> *rebellion is as the sin of witchcraft, and*
> *stubbornness is as iniquity and idolatry.*
> *Because thou hast rejected the word of the*
> *LORD, he hath also rejected thee from*
> *being king.*

1 Samuel 15:23

Disobedience was a constant problem for Saul. When God made it clear that David would be the next king, Saul didn't accept the Lord's will. Instead, he tried to hunt down David to kill him. It seems prescient that Samuel equated Saul's rebellion with witchcraft, because here at the end of Saul's life, the king throws away everything he knows to be right and goes to consult a medium.

Saul's servants inform him that a medium lives in Endor, a town between Mount Tabor and the Hill of Moreh in the Jezreel Valley. She has managed to survive the purge, and she's a mistress of necromancy – one who consults the dead to determine the future. Now, the punishment for mediums and consulting mediums is death, and the witch knows this. Saul should have remembered it as well, because this penalty is dealt against Saul the very next day in the Valley of Jezreel.

Saul dresses himself up and disguises himself so he won't be recognized as the king, and he asks this medium to bring up a familiar spirit. She protests that he's setting her up to be executed, because King Saul has made all those kinds of activities illegal. He reassures her that she won't get in trouble, so she asks him whom it is he wants to speak to, and he says, "Samuel." She goes to bring up Samuel, and when she sees him, she's shocked and cries out with a loud voice!

This might indicate that the woman was generally a charlatan, because she apparently wasn't expecting to really see Samuel. When the old man appears to her, she yells. Maybe the witch had a normal spirit she depended on, and that spirit didn't appear; Samuel appeared instead.

Now we've got a problem right here. Whom did the witch at Endor really see? Was it Samuel himself pulled up from his temporary rest in Sheol, or was it a demon impersonating Samuel? On one hand, all the woman did was describe an old man in a mantle, and Saul "perceived" it was Samuel. On the other hand, the things Samuel say certainly sound correct. It's possible that we have here a genuine appearance of Samuel that God himself brought about. At the very least, the following prophecy by Samuel came true the next day.

> *And Samuel said to Saul, Why hast thou*
> *disquieted me, to bring me up? And Saul*
> *answered, I am sore distressed; for the*
> *Philistines make war against me, and*
> *God is departed from me, and answereth*
> *me no more, neither by prophets, nor by*
> *dreams: therefore I have called thee, that*
> *thou mayest make known unto me what*
> *I shall do. Then said Samuel, Wherefore*
> *then dost thou ask of me, seeing the LORD*
> *is departed from thee, and is become thine*
> *enemy? And the LORD hath done to him,*
> *as he spake by me: for the LORD hath rent*
> *the kingdom out of thine hand, and given*
> *it to thy neighbour, even to David: Because*
> *thou obeyedst not the voice of the LORD,*
> *nor executedst his fierce wrath upon*
> *Amalek, therefore hath the LORD done*
> *this thing unto thee this day. Moreover the*

> *LORD will also deliver Israel with thee*
> *into the hand of the Philistines: and to*
> *morrow shalt thou and thy sons be with*
> *me: the LORD also shall deliver the host of*
> *Israel into the hand of the Philistines.*
>
> 1 Samuel 28:15-19

Now, while Satan is the accuser of the brethren, and it might have pleased a demon to give Saul this bad news, the Bible does identify this person as Samuel in several places. That's interesting.

After it's over, Saul is upset, but the medium kills a calf and feeds Saul meat and bread. Then he and his servants leave to return to the battlefield, where Saul will die the next day along with his sons.

It's also interesting that Samuel never answers Saul's initial question about what he should do. The harsh reality is that there's nothing Saul can do because of his disobedience. The battle that follows the next day at Mount Gilboa in 1 Samuel 31 is a disaster. From the beginning, Saul's army is routed and slaughtered, including his sons. Saul is wounded by an arrow, and he asks his armor bearer to thrust him through with a sword and kill him. The armor bearer won't do it, so Saul manages to fall on his own sword in an effort to kill himself. When the Philistines find Saul's body, they dishonor him by cutting off his head, stripping his armor, and hanging his naked body on the wall in the open square.

The great disgrace of Saul was not in how the Philistines treated his body, it was his lack of obedience to the will and the word of God. As we read his story, though, we all know that we could easily be in Saul's place. We have all been guilty of direct disobedience to God. We've all decided we were going to do things our own way instead of His. We fear people rather than fearing the Lord, and if we're honest with ourselves, we might have saved some of the best of the spoil from that battle with the Amalekites, just as Saul did.

Are we like Saul? Would we chase the witches and mediums out of the land, only to turn to them in a moment of desperation? Are we willing to say, "Yes, seeking knowledge or power through the occult is wrong," in one minute, but then take in a Tarot card reading the next?

Most importantly, how do we take care of our children? At Halloween, we don't want them exposed to ideas and experiences that could open them up to spiritual invasion. Do we teach them well, or do we just give in and let them do whatever?

Chapter 13
UFOs

There is one last dimension of the occult that I want to address: aliens. Audiences love aliens, and interest in UFOs has sold millions of copies of books. It's not that UFOs don't exist. I'm convinced they do. The real issue is what and who they are, and why they are zipping in and out of sight in the sky all around the world.

It's hard to debunk UFOs, and researchers who have tried often end up committed to their reality. We cannot dismiss all UFOs as hallucinations. When they appear, crowds of witnesses can see them together. They're not imaginary. They're real. They leave tangible evidence, like scorched ground, and their presence can be picked up by our instruments just like other aircraft. However, UFOs also tend to defy physical laws. They take right angles at high speeds, and as I've read some of the stories, it seems that they are physical, but *not* physical at the same time.

Several of our astronauts have confirmed UFO sightings on their missions. On November 3, 1978, Major Gordon Cooper from the Mercury program wrote a letter to Ambassador Griffith of the Mission of Grenada to the United Nations, making suggestions about the issue of UFOs. Cooper believed these were extra-terrestrials and we needed to take steps to maintain peace with these beings. He stated in part:

> I believe that these extra-terrestrial vehicles and their crews are visiting this planet from other planets, which obviously are a little more technically advanced than we are here on earth...I do feel that I am somewhat qualified to discuss them since I have been into the fringes of the vast areas in which they travel. Also, I did have occasion in 1951 to have two days of observation of many flights of them, of different sizes, flying in fighter formation, generally from east to west over Europe. They were at a higher altitude than we could reach with our jet fighters of that time.

According to National UFO Reporting Center data, the yearly number of reported sightings remained below 5,000 per year until 1980, when the number began to spike – from 10,000 per year in 1990 up to 42,000 per year in 2000. In 2010 there were approximately 45,000 UFO sightings reported.[45] They come in the shape of saucers and the shape of cigars, as big orbs or as mysterious lights. The ease of access to the Internet might be a factor in the increased rate of reporting, since it's much easier to find out how to report UFOs these days, and everybody carries a camera in their pockets. It may also be that the number of UFO incidents is just plain increasing.

For a long time, these experiences were regarded as hallucinations or incidents in which people made a big deal out of something easily explained, like experimental military craft or weather balloons or swamp gas. However, a significant number of recorded instances defy any reasonable naturalistic explanation. People who have reported UFOs have moved from the lunatic fringe – as they were regarded in the 1950s – to a source of common themes in entertainment. The research confirms that whatever UFOs are, they are real. They are caught on camera and radar. Sometimes large multitudes of people witness an event together. In the summer of 1996, a multitude of sighting reports poured in across Israel, not just from Israeli citizens, but the police and army as well. On August 4, 1996 in Eilat, Israel, more than a thousand people watched as an enormous UFO traveled slowly over the city, then split in two and disappeared.[46]

One-time Navy pilot Cmdr. David Fravor described a UFO he observed in 2004 off the coast of California after it and others had descended from 80,000 feet. He told *The Washington Post* he saw an object "40 feet long with no wings, just hanging close to the water." He told the *Post*, "As I get closer, as my nose is starting to pull back up, it accelerates and it's gone. Faster than I'd ever seen anything in my life. We turn around, say let's go see what's in the water and there's nothing. Just blue water."[47]

Fravor defended himself to ABC News, saying, "I can tell you, I think it was not from this world. I'm not crazy, haven't been drinking. It was — after 18 years of flying, I've seen pretty much about everything that I can see in that realm, and this was nothing close."[48]

The question is, what are they? The evidence points to deceptive interdimensional beings, and I think they're demonic. These unidentified spacecraft have some interesting characteristics. They perform feats that appear to defy the laws of physics. They take off at speeds faster than we can manage, changing directions without inertial effects, and sometimes they just plain disappear.

"You know, you see a lot of interesting things," Fravor told *ABC News*. "But to show up on something that's a 40-foot-long white Tic Tac with no wings that can move, really, in any random direction that it wants and go from hovering over the ocean to mirroring us to accelerating to the point where it just disappears — like, poof, then it was gone."[49]

People often assume that these types of things are extra-terrestrial aliens from another part of the galaxy, but we find as we investigate further that they tend to exhibit strange and deceptive behavior. I don't have the space to do justice to these things here, but we do cover them in-depth in our book *Alien Encounters*.[50]

Remember the strange goings-on in the days before Noah, when the fallen angels were producing offspring with the human women. These angels were the bad guys, apostate angels, and they mated with the women and produced the *Nephilim*, Hebrew for "fallen ones."[51] The Nephilim were giants, and I believe part of the purpose of the Flood was to wipe out these monster beings. The myths of ancient cultures also embody the memory of these things through their legends, as in the Greek titans.

What happened to those angels that sinned, who left their glorious heavenly bodies and took on the form of humans in order to mate with the women? Peter and Jude both tell us they are chained up in the lowest hell awaiting the day of judgment.[52]

It's notable that the word "Tartarus" is used in 2 Peter 2:4 alone in the New Testament as the word for "hell." Tartarus is used in Homer, and in the Greek, Tartarus was viewed as being as far below hell as hell was below the earth. It's the lowest part of hell, and that's where we find chained up those angels that left their first habitation. They are there, waiting for their eternal judgment.

We hear of today's aliens kidnapping people and doing odd experiments on them, often of a sexual nature. It wouldn't surprise me if these were the same sorts of beings, but with a new face for a technological world.

We know that there is a great deception coming, one that will appeal to people of the modern era. The UFO phenomenon provides a useful front for the great deceivers. In the ancient days, people worshiped the stars and entities that came down from the stars as beings of light. Shirley MacClaine talks to "star people." Those who would never attend a séance due to unbelief might embrace the idea of extra-terrestrial life. Stephen Hawking thought it was reasonable to believe that life exists elsewhere in the universe, and Neil DeGrasse Tyson has proved willing to speculate on alien civilizations and what it might be like if they came here. Many scientists fail to see the evidence for God, but they recognize there are a multitude of suns out in the universe with the potential for planets that have evolved life.

Human beings seek to answer a very basic question: "Is there more to life than this?" When people reject God, it's easy to fall back on alien life as the answer to that question. Are we alone? No, these hopefuls speculate. No, there is probably life elsewhere in the universe. One of the great deceptive ideas circling through the West is that we were brought here by aliens, that we are the result of seeding by an alien race. Efforts to explain the origin of life on Earth have proved problematic, to say the least. However, if there wasn't time or materials to have evolved life here, people contemplate that perhaps life evolved somewhere else and was brought here.

This speculation provides the spiritual enemies of God a superb disguise for additional deception. The Word of God promises massive delusions in the end times. The masses will believe the lie. Which lie? The lie that denies the Creator and denies the redemption that He has made available through His Son. It might easily be the lie that an alien civilization is the true source of our existence as well as the source of greater knowledge, the source of truth, and a strong leadership toward world peace.

In late 2017, *The New York Times* ran an article claiming that the Pentagon had spent years investigating the UFO phenomenon at the behest of one-time Senate Majority Leader Harry Reid, who allegedly grew interested in UFO research on the urging of astronaut John Glenn. According to the article, the program money primarily went to an aerospace research company run by Harry Reid's billionaire friend Robert Bigelow. The article makes the following statement:

> *Working with Mr. Bigelow's Las Vegas-based company, the program produced documents that describe sightings of aircraft that seemed to move at very high velocities with no visible signs of propulsion, or that hovered with no apparent means of lift.*[53]

The New York Times reminds us of Project Blue Book, in which the U.S. Airforce spent 17 years between 1952 and 1969 investigating 12,000 UFO sightings and found natural, reasonable explanations for all but 701. It goes on to describe the success of Harry Reid's more recent program, quoting Mr. Reid in a letter to then-deputy defense secretary William Lynn III as saying, "Much progress has been made with the identification of several highly sensitive, unconventional aerospace-related findings." The implications are that exceptionally high-tech materials have been recovered – though the article doesn't give us specifics.

New York Magazine soon commented on the public reaction to the *Times* article, remarking:

> The news that aliens might actually be visiting us, regularly and recently, didn't provoke terror about a coming space-opera conflict but something much more like the Evangelical dream of the Rapture the same liberals might have mocked as kooky right-wing escapism in the George W. Bush years. "The truth is out there,: former senator Harry Reid tweeted, with a link to the story. Thank God, came the response through the Twitter vent. "Could extraterrestrials help us save Earth" went one typical reaction.[54]

There are many indications that the so-called aliens that have visited our planet are nothing of the sort. It's not simply that their spacecraft defy the laws of physics, that they can appear and disappear at will. We find that those who have had encounters with these beings describe a message that is unbiblical.

A multitude of websites can be found that describe alleged UFO sightings and aliens and alien encounters. It's particularly interesting the spiritual aspect that appears at some of these sites. The Internet is not the source for solid, trustworthy information, but it does offer us insight into attitudes. For instance, TruthSeekah. com describes the views of a David Curtis that the aliens are guides, much like religion's view of angels. While bringing up the Holy Spirit and God, the TruthSeekah.com site expresses the situation in very New Age terms stating:

> David speaks about summoning UFOs and making contact with aliens or interdimensional beings through meditation…Many people are starting to feel that these so called aliens or visitors from above are simply what we would call the angels from our own religious texts. This episode shows us that there is something deeper to be found within our experiences because we are not alone and never have been all along.

This is the heart of the issue. These beings can be accessed through spiritual means. They are not merely physical beings who have traveled through space and time to do experiments on us. They are interdimensional beings, and we even find cases of possession.

A 2009 film called *The Fourth Kind* dramatizes events involving "aliens" that possessed the people of Nome, Alaska in 2000. I don't recommend it, but I do want to note the parallel between aliens and demons provided by this film. A psychologist named Abbey Tyler used hypnosis on townspeople to draw out supposed repressed memories of alien abductions. Children have disappeared, and the parents are convinced they've been taken by aliens. Yet, the alien that apparently kidnapped Abbey's daughter refers to itself as the savior and father, and ends with "I am …God." The movie reproduces videos taken of individuals as they levitated and contorted horribly and spoke with guttural voices in ancient Sumerian.

The devils that sought to damage and destroy people in the time of Jesus are still around, and they still seek to damage and destroy. They've just put on a different mask.

What do we do about it? Studying is insufficient. Intellect, no matter how powerful it is, no matter how well-informed we are, will not help us avoid being deceived. Why? Because all this is a spiritual battle and not an intellectual exercise. It's a spiritual battle. Jesus told us that there would be false Christs and false prophets that, if it were possible, would deceive the very elect.[55] The Holy Spirit and the Bible reveal the truth, and greater is He who is in us than he who is in the world.[56] UFO experiences, the occultic experiences on the planet Earth today, widespread as they are, remain relatively underground for now. The evil god of this world, however, is planning his ultimate end-time deception, and I wouldn't be surprised if aliens coming to save the world will play a part.

Chapter 14
Our Heavy Artillery

The ultimate question in all of this is, "What do we do?" How do we approach Halloween, especially when we have children and teenagers involved? There are clearly a variety of alternative diversions that Christians can take on Halloween, from harvest parties to praise and worship. There's another idea I have long liked. The kids can create a pageant in which they act out the story of Saul and the Witch of Endor from 1 Samuel 28, which doesn't end well for Saul. They might also act out a play on Martin Luther, and the focus of the day can be on how the Reformation started. This approach encourages the kids to learn about these things, and they have the opportunity to express all their creativity and energy in a positive way at the end of October.

In the 1990s, we ran a national contest to write a play for Saul and the Witch of Endor, and we received a multitude of entries. A panel of judges chaired by Frank Peretti read through the entries and picked the four best plays, which we still offer for free to the public.[57] A fifth play has been added to the original four, and we welcome and encourage you to take advantage of these scripts.

Pick the one that best suits your particular group of youths and have the kids create a play that can be performed Halloween night. It's fun, and it provides the opportunity to teach the kids about the dangers of the occult.

If your group desires something a little more erudite, I encourage you to track down a copy of *The lady is Not for Burning* by Christopher Fry. It's just a secular play, but it's provocative. There are many possibilities for entertainment and education during the time of year that has been so constantly dedicated to witches and zombies and demons. I think the main purpose is to find ways to attack the problem, and Halloween is a good time of year to address the very real dangers of messing with occultic activities. It's a dangerous time of year, but it's also a valuable time for witnessing. The spirit world is real, after all.

We live on a spiritual battlefield. We are in the middle of a constant battle for the lives of human beings, but Christ already has the victory. That's the important thing to remember. He's armed us with heavy artillery, and we are not defenseless. We simply need to be wise and not go walking unarmed into enemy territory.

Satan attempts to counterfeit the real power we have through Christ Jesus. We are heirs of God, and we have access to the power and infilling of the Holy Spirit of God, and greater is He that is in us than He that is in the world.[58] If we are in Jesus Christ, we have Him dwelling in us. If we walk with His Spirit and obey Him, we can have great victory over the enemy. We can route him and chase him out of our homes and our communities. The Spirit of God dwells in the praises of His people, and if we dedicate ourselves to Him and fight the good fight, we can beat this evil thing that has been attempting to take over our lives.

We cannot just sit back on our laurels. We need to do our spiritual homework and arm ourselves. Which leads us to Ephesians 6:

> *Finally, my brethren, be strong in the Lord, and in the power of his might. Put on the whole armour of God, that ye may be able to stand against the wiles of the devil. For we wrestle not against flesh and blood, but against principalities, against powers, against the rulers of the darkness of this world, against spiritual wickedness in high places. Wherefore take unto you the whole armour of God, that ye may be able to withstand in the evil day, and having done all, to stand. Stand therefore, having your loins girt about with truth, and having on the breastplate of righteousness; And your feet shod with the preparation of the gospel of peace; Above all, taking the shield of faith, wherewith ye shall be able to quench all the fiery darts of the wicked. And take the helmet of salvation, and the sword of the Spirit, which is the word of God: Praying always*

with all prayer and supplication in the
Spirit, and watching thereunto with all
perseverance and supplication for all saints;

Ephesians 6:10-18

Put on the whole armor of God. When do we do that? After the battle has started? No, we do it right now, because we're already on enemy territory. Those principalities and powers and rulers of darkness are hosts of demons, some of them extremely powerful. There is spiritual wickedness in high places, but we can beat them back and reclaim territory for the Lord. We need to understand this armor He's provided for us and how to wear it.

What does it mean to wear the belt of truth? Having one's loins girded meant being able to run without tripping. The warriors tucked their robes up into their belts, which freed their legs for running. 1 Peter 1:13 tells us to gird up the loins of our mind. We have to start with the truth so we don't trip and fall.

The breastplate protected the vital area, the heart and lungs. If we get stabbed through the heart, that's fatal, so we need to put on Christ's righteousness as a breastplate. It's the same with the helmet of salvation that protects our head. It's His armor, it's His righteousness that protects us. It's His salvation.

We need our feet shod with the preparation of the Gospel of peace. Our shoes and footwork are essential. As 1 Peter 3:15 encourages us, we need to be always ready to give a reason for the hope within us.

Above all, we need to take the shield of faith, trusting that God is who He says He is. He is faithful. He is trustworthy. He is holy and righteous. He loves us massively and deeply.

We are on enemy territory, and we need to always be ready. If there are holes in our armor, we need to get those fixed before we go into battle. If our shield of faith is damaged, we need to go and get that fixed by doing our biblical homework and seeking the help of God. He wants us well-armored.

We sometimes feel that we are on the defense all the time, that we are constantly under attack. We don't have to be. We can be on the offensive. We also have the Sword of the Spirit, which is the Word of God, and we need to know how to wield this sword. Of course, that means knowing God's Word. We have to know what it says inside and out, otherwise we won't even know how to swing our weapon. The sword of the Romans was a short, double-edged close quarters combat sword. Almost like a large dagger. The Word of God is powerful and sharp, like a double-edged sword, and it has a way of hacking through the garbage. Hebrews 4:12 tells us that it is a *"discerner of the thoughts and intents of the heart."*

Remember, when Satan tempted Jesus in the wilderness in Luke 4, Jesus didn't combat Satan using brilliant logic and philosophical arguments.

Jesus simple responded to Satan by saying, "*It is written.*" It's easy to recognize when a bit of teaching is erroneous when we already know the truth.

Paul finishes up with our heavy artillery: prayer. This is often left out of these teachings on the armor of God, but it's exceptionally important. When we pray, God works. It's like calling in fire from the ships out in the harbor: it's action at a distance. Whenever we are engaged in a battle with the enemy, prayer with praise and thanksgiving is a powerful resource that can tear down the enemy's strongholds.

The enemy has real strongholds. It can have dominion over buildings or towns or even countries, about which Daniel 10 gives us clues. By the power of God working through us, however, God can go before us and tear down those strongholds and establish His dominion instead. The battle is held in our prayer closet, and we truly do have victory through Christ Jesus.

We just can't give up. Sometimes it takes time to tear down the enemy's walls, but if we hammer and hammer and hammer with the artillery that God has given us, those spiritual walls will eventually crumble down.

The enemy will fire back. Don't think he won't, because he's fighting for his life. He will attack, and that means that we need to place our homes and family members under the protection of the blood of Christ. If Satan can't go after us, he'll go after our family members, but we can also keep them bathed in a protection of daily prayer.

We can pray for our families and our communities, our local schools and our local government. We can pray for our states and state governments and for the members of the Executive, Legislative, and Judicial branches of our government. If we want our country to be spiritually healthy, we are responsible to take it to the enemy every day through prayer. The words of God in the day of Solomon are as true today as they ever were:

> *If my people, which are called by my*
> *name, shall humble themselves, and pray,*
> *and seek my face, and turn from their*
> *wicked ways; then will I hear from heaven,*
> *and will forgive their sin, and will heal*
> *their land.*

2 Chronicles 7:14

If we are concerned about the rise of the occult in our country, the rise of deception and lies that threaten to drag people into hell, then we can do something about it. It doesn't start with the occultists. It starts with us. We are called by the name of Jesus Christ. We need to humble ourselves and pray and turn from our wicked ways. It starts right here in our homes, in our lives, in our churches. If we do this, then God promises that He will hear and He will heal our land.

Let's bow our hearts.

Father, we are so grateful that You dwell in us, and that You are greater than the evil rulers of this world. Thank You that we are already more than conquerors through Christ who loves us. Father, we ask that You blind the forces of darkness that are threatening to overwhelm us and put them in confusion. The forces of darkness desire to terrify us, Father, but we take refuge in Jesus Christ. Thank You that You have provided us with a redemption that's available for the asking. We pray, Father, that every one of us would reject specifically before Your throne any of the involvements we've had with the occult in whatever form, that we might be truly freed from those entanglements. We confess these things as sin, Father, and we reject and refute them before Your Throne. We deny Satan and all his works and all his ways. Father, thank You for our salvation by the shed blood of Jesus Christ; we want You to take over our lives, that through the ministry of Your Holy Spirit we might be equipped to be effective for You. Thank You for Your overwhelming love, Father. Thank You for the freedom and protection that You offer us, even while we walk through the valley of the shadow of death. Father, please give us wisdom, give us insight into the enemy's schemes, that we can be as wise as serpents and remain innocent as doves. Please help us to put on Your armor, that we can be fully equipped to be warriors for You, that Your purposes would be accomplished in each of our lives. We long for You, Father, and we are forever grateful that You have made us – not just Your servants – but Your children and heirs.

Father, we look forward to the day when we can dwell with You in Your Kingdom. We commit ourselves before You in the name of Yeshua Ha'Maschiach, our Lord and Savior Jesus Christ. Amen.

Endnotes

1 - National Retail Federation, "Halloween Spending to Reach 9 Billion." September 20, 2018. https://nrf.com/media-center/press-releases/halloween-spending-reach-9-billion, last accessed December 20, 2018.

2 - Julius Caesar, *Gallic War*, VI.14.

3 - *Ibid*, VI.16.

4 - Tacitus, *Annals*, XIV.30.

5 - Strabo, *Geography*, IV.4.5.

6 - Diodorus Siculus, *Library of History*, V:31.3.

7 - John 3:16, 14:6; Acts 4:12; 1 Peter 1:18, 19; 1 John 1:7

8 - Cf. Patten, Donald, Hatch, Ronald, & Steinhauer Loren. *The Long Day of Joshua and Six Other Catastrophes* (Seattle: Pacific Meridian), 1973.

9 - Missler, Chuck. *The Mysteries of the Planet Mars* (Coeur d'Alene: Koinonia House), 1996.

10 - 2 Kings 20:8-12; Isaiah 38:8

11 - Shakespeare, William. *Macbeth*, Act I, Scene 3, Lines 122-126.

12 - 1 Peter 5:8

13 - Martin, Walter, Martin Rische, Jill, and Van Gorden, Kurt. *The Kingdom of the Occult* (Nashville: Thomas Nelson, 213-214), 2008.

14 - 1 John 4:8

15 - Psalm 16:11

16 - Isaiah 9:6

17 - Gecewicz, Clair. "New Age' beliefs common among both religious and nonreligious Americans." Pew

Research, October 1, 2018.

18 - Bischoff, R.A., ed. *The Lutheran Pioneer: A Missionary Monthly*, (St. Louis: Evangelical Lutheran Synodical Conference of North America, 12), March 1879

19 - As quoted in Reeves, Michael and Chester, Tim. Why the Reformation Still Matters. (Wheaton, IL:Crossway), 2016.

20 - Philippians 1:23

21 - Acts 7:59

22 - 2 Peter 2:9

23 - 2 Peter 2:4

24 - Jude 1:6

25 - 2 Corinthians 5:8

26 - Mark 5:1-20; 7:25-30; Luke 9:38-42

27 - Luke 8:33

28 - John 1:1-5, 10-14.

29 - Bayard, Louis. "Shirley MacLaine recalls the sinking of Atlantis and other past-life challenges." *The Washington Post*, February 27, 2016.

30 - Cf. Matthew 15:22-28, 17:14-18; Mar 9:17-29; Acts 16:16-18.

31 - I'm indebted to Gayle Erwin for showing me this poem at a men's conference.

32 - Revelation 20:10

33 - 2 Corinthians 11:14

34 - Luke 10:18

35 - John 12:31, 14:30, 16:11

36 - Revelation 12:9

37 - Matthew 12:26-28

38 - Revelation 12:12

39 - Ephesians 2:2

40 - Please see our books, *Angels Volume I: Cosmic Warfare and Angels Volume II: Messengers From The Metacosm.*

41 - Ephesians 2:1-2

42 - Revelation 12:10

43 - Matthew 4:8-10; Luke 4:5-8

44 - 1 Samuel 27.

45 - Fox News. "UFO sightings hit all-time high, report says." *Fox News*, February 28, 2017.

46 - *UFO Reality*, Issue 6, February/March 1997, p.10-11.

47 - Rosenberg, Eli. "Former navy pilot describes encounter with UFO studied by secretive Pentagon program." *The Washington Post*, December 18, 2017.

48 - McCarthy, Kelly. "Navy pilot recalls encounter with UFO: 'I think it was not from this world'" *ABC News*, December 18, 2017.

49 - *Ibid.*

50 - Eastman, Mark and Missler, Chuck. *Alien Encounters*, (Coeur d'Alene: Koinonia House) 1997.

51 - For more information on this subject, see the 2003 update of our study *The Return of the Nephilim.*

52 - 2 Peter 2:4; Jude 1:6

53 - Cooper, Helene, Blumenthal, Ralph, and Kean, Leslie. "Glowing Auras and 'Black Money': The Pentagon's Mysterious U.F.O. Program. *The New York Times.* December 16, 2017.

54 - Wallace-Wells, David, et al. "Reasons to Believe: How seriously should you take those recent reports of

UFOs? Ask the Pentagon. Or read this primer for the SETI-curious." *New York Magazine*, March 20, 2018.

55 - Matthew 24:24; Mark 13:22.

56 - I John 4:4

57 - These can be found at the K-House website: www. khouse.org by doing a search for "Halloween plays." As of this writing, they are available at https:// khouse.org/pages/halloween_plays/.

58 - 1 John 4:4.

About the Author

Chuck Missler
Founder, Koinonia House

Chuck Missler was raised in Southern California.

Chuck demonstrated an aptitude for technical interests as a youth. He became a ham radio operator at age nine and started piloting airplanes as a teenager. While still in high school, Chuck built a digital computer in the family garage.

His plans to pursue a doctorate in electrical engineering at Stanford University were interrupted when he received a Congressional appointment to the United States Naval Academy at Annapolis. Graduating with honors, Chuck took his commission in the Air Force. After completing flight training, he met and married Nancy (who later founded The King's High Way Ministries). Chuck joined the Missile Program and eventually became Branch Chief of the Department of Guided Missiles at Lowry Air Force Base.

Chuck made the transition from the military to the private sector when he became a systems engineer with TRW, a large aerospace firm. He then went on to serve as a senior analyst with a non-profit think tank where he conducted projects for the intelligence community and the Department of Defense. During that time, Chuck earned a master's degree in engineering at UCLA, supplementing previous graduate work in applied mathematics, advanced statistics and information sciences.

Recruited into senior management at the Ford Motor Company in Dearborn, Michigan, Chuck established the first international computer network in 1966. He left Ford to start his own company, a computer network firm that was subsequently acquired by Automatic Data Processing (listed on the New York Stock Exchange) to become its Network Services Division.

As Chuck noted, his day of reckoning came in the early '90s when — as the result of a merger — he found himself the chairman and a major shareholder of a small, publicly owned development company known as Phoenix Group International. The firm established an $8 billion joint venture with the Soviet Union to supply personal computers to their 143,000 schools. Due to several unforeseen circumstances, the venture failed. The Misslers lost everything, including their home, automobiles and insurance.

It was during this difficult time that Chuck turned to God and the Bible. As a child he had developed an intense interest in the Bible; studying it became a favorite pastime. In the 1970s, while still in the corporate world, Chuck began leading weekly Bible studies at the 30,000 member Calvary Chapel Costa Mesa, in California. He and Nancy established Koinonia House in 1973, an organization devoted to encouraging people to study the Bible.

Chuck had enjoyed a longtime, personal relationship with Hal Lindsey, who upon hearing of Chuck's professional misfortune, convinced him that he could easily succeed as an independent author and speaker. Over the years, Chuck had developed a loyal following. (Through Doug Wetmore, head of the tape ministry of Firefighters for Christ, Chuck learned that over 7 million copies of his taped Bible studies were scattered throughout the world.) Koinonia House then became Chuck's full-time profession until his retirement in 2017.

In May, 2018, Chuck passed away peacefully at his home in Reporoa, New Zealand.

Hidden Treasures

For the novice, as well as the sophisticate, this book is full of surprises. It includes subtle discoveries lying just "beneath" the text – hidden messages, encryptions, deliberate misspellings and other amendments to the text – that present implications beyond the immediate context, demonstrating a skillful design that has its origin from outside our space and time. Drawing upon over forty years of collecting, Chuck highlights in this book many of the precious nuggets that have become characteristic of his popular Bible studies around the world.

It is guaranteed to stimulate, provoke, and, hopefully, to disturb. It will confound the skeptic and encourage the believer. It is a "must read" for every thinking seeker of truth and serious inquirer of reality.

Hidden Treasures
IN THE BIBLICAL TEXT
Chuck Missler

It is the glory of God
to conceal a matter;
It is the honor of kings
to search out a matter.

For pro... old tim... not in but ho... of man, as they... spoke ...by the Holy Spirit.

I have also ...en by the prophets, ...ave multiplied visions, and have used similitudes by the ministry

Learn the Bible

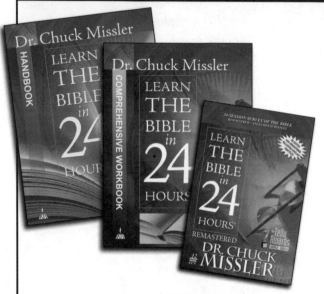

Are you ready for a detailed yet thoroughly enjoyable study of the most profound book ever written?

Using sound scientific facts, historical analysis, and Biblical narrative, acclaimed teacher Dr. Chuck Missler weaves together a rich tapestry of information—providing an accurate understanding of Scripture's relation to itself, to us and to the world at large.

Examine the heroic tales of Exodus, the lasting wisdom of Proverbs, or even the enigmatic imagery of Revelation with the simple, Scripturally sound insights and fresh perspectives found in *Learn the Bible in 24 Hours*. Whether you want to explore some of the less-discussed nuances of Scripture or you need a comprehensive refresher course on the Bible's themes and stories, *Learn the Bible in 24 Hours* is a great guide.

How We Got Our Bible

- Where did our Bible come from? How good are the texts?
- Why do we believe its origin is supernatural?
- How do we know that it really is the Word of God?
- How accurate are our translations?
- Which version is the best?

Chuck Missler, an internationally recognized Biblical authority, reviews the origin of both the Old and New Testaments in light of recent discoveries and controversies.

How We Got Our Bible

DR. CHUCK MISSLER